Bring Back The Whigs

…and Other Modest Proposals to Fix Political Funk

Jack Adler

W & B Publishers
United States

Bring Back The Whigs ...and Other Modest Proposals to Fix Political Funk © 2013. All rights reserved by Jack Adler

No part of this book may be reproduced or transmitted in any form or by any means, graphic, electronic, or mechanical, including photocopying, recording, taping, or by any informational storage retrieval system without prior permission in writing from the publisher.

A-Argus Better Book Publishers, LLC

For information:
A-Argus Better Book Publishers, LLC
9001 Ridge Hill Street
Kernersville, North Carolina 27285
www.a-argusbooks.com

ISBN: 978-0-6159311-7-3
ISBN: 0-6159311-7-0

Book Cover designed by Dubya

Printed in the United States of America

Dedication

Dedicated to honest and conscientious politicians everywhere. May they survive and the people prosper!

Bring Back The Whigs
...and Other Modest Proposals to Fix Political Funk

Table of Contents

1. Politicare
2. Gridlock Video
3. Military Names
4. Offensive Humor Calculator
5. Bring Back The Whigs
6. Public Pulpit, Limp Pulpit
7. Catch 22 Concentrate
8. Apps Away
9. It's Job, Stupid
10. Latter Day Humiliation
11. Baseball Drug League
12. Revisionism, American Style
13. Political Privatization
14. Quarter The Veterans
15. Vote/Dine/Shop
16. Entitlements in Person
17. 24/7 News Syndrome
18. Political Awards Ceremony
19. Political Families
20. Marital Bliss, Corporate
21. National Hysteria Index
22. Worldwide Volunteer Army
23. Punditry
24. Sister Couples
25. Dictators & Education
26. Reforming The Draft
27. Youth & Politics
28. Renditions In Revise
29. Culture War Champions
30. Designated President Rule
31. American Sharia

32. Immigration Reversed
33. Reconciliation U.S.A.
34. GRIN – Gambling On Inflation
35. American Exceptionalism
36. Senior Commandos
37. Plea Bargaining Club
38. SON – Stop Obesity Now
39. Mandatory Bicycle Use
40. Predisposition To Terrorism
41. Of Pickpockets & Oil Magnates
42. Philanthropy Mandate
43. Political Scandal Fund
44. Divorce Tax
45. Dollar Insurance
46. Political Contribution Cure
47. Presidential Pardons
48. Pledge Of Allegiance Amended
49. CCEP – Concerned Citizens For Ex-Presidents
50. Political Courage Test
51. "Street Smarts" Course
52. Dike America
53. Arabica Television Channel
54. Expanding Commonwealth
55. Political Paychecks, Sartorially
56. American Madrasahs
57. Military Morale Boosters
58. Senior Day
59. Of Cities & Television
60. Verbalists
61. Moratorium On Lawyers
62. CREATE
63. Theme Park/Balance Of Payments
64. Comic Brainstorm Routings – The New CBR
65. Supreme Court Adjustment
66. New President Day, New Congress Day
67. Gerrymandering Derailed

68. Medical Globalization
69. Journalists Shield
70. American Highways In Africa
71. Socialism & Communism Defanged
72. Signing Statements
73. Spins/Half-Truths
74. Geographical & Linguistic Literacy
75. America Disarmed
76. School For Benign Dictators
77. Ban Bullets, Not Guns
78. Corporate Luxury Tax On Salaries
79. Disinformation Dissected
80. Filibuster Failure
81. Confound Phone Marketers
82. Political Labelitis
83. Political Pledges
84. A "Nothing" Museum
85. Mental Health Centers
86. New Tort: Mental Adverse Possession
87. False Inspiration From Books
88. Taking A Political Break
89. Minimum Wage Blues
90. Political Betting Pools
91. National Shun Association
92. Celebrity Monarchy
93. EA Or Emotional Age
94. The New Machismo
95. Outdated Movie/TV Scenes
96. Home "Know Thyself" Kit
97. Index of Dubious Items
98. Asymmetric Peace
99. Be A Futurist
100. American Deathnauts

Jack Adler

1. Politicare

Pity our poor politicians. Raging partisanship and the contagious political disease sometimes called "Gotcha" have placed an entire generation of politicians under the threat of scandals, forced resignations, impeachment, and even imprisonment. Many politicians have been accused of lesser sins such as lack of courage and voting for their party instead of by their conscience, or even the collective will of their constituents. Now, more than ever, there is a realistic need for legislation that can relieve some of the anxieties politicians may face.

Such a much needed bill would be designed to offer relief to politicians who have been deposed for a variety of reasons including resignations under fire and outright dismissal. One of the more recent examples is Scooter Libby, chief of staff to Vice President Dick Cheney; but former cases take in President Nixon and other Watergate figures as well as Vice President Spiro Agnew. Unfortunately, a new slew of candidates – from municipal to federal levels of governance - are always possibilities.

Here are suggested rudiments of "Politicare," a measure to help dispel the negative opinions many people have today of politicians and to help the ousted politician or federal official for the rest of his or her life. The fact that ex-presidents get federal-mandated protection doesn't in any way ameliorate or remove the sting of national disgrace. After all, it isn't always easy for this type of person, still in the public eye, to find a new or respected niche in life.

Not all the provisions of such a measure have been ironed out yet, but there would be a special rehabilitation and educational program with credibility courses and instruction in such subjects as personal ethics, credible subjects for speeches, and memoir-material selection. No matter how well fixed they are, or how good their connections are, it's a whole new ballgame to these victims of their own malfeasance.

The program would be administered by the federal government in association with the states. While some states might not initially want to participate, possibly over shame about the fall from grace of their native sons and daughters, a publicity campaign is likely to sway their attitude. The element of possible rehabilitation of such high-level personages can have a good deal of appeal to moral-minded state legislators.

One of the problems with such a putative program is determining the degree of need of the particular politician. It's embarrassing for some of them to admit they're in any sort of distress. Provisions also need to be sorted out on what portion of the program is federally or state funded, and whether one has to be an elected official or not to be a candidate. It's also vital to establish at what level in the government hierarchy such help would kick in.

From a different perspective, it may be necessary to educate the public on the need for such a program. Members of the public may lack enough sympathy for these ex-politicians to want their tax money used for this purpose. The public is rightfully dubious about politicians and that factor has to be taken into consideration. Such a bill should certainly not be retroactive. Still up for discussion is whether any personal expenditures on the part of individuals, in relation to the program, can be used as income tax deductions.

On the latter score, many favor making funding to come from a voluntary contribution item on income tax forms. But if not enough money is raised on a voluntary basis, it will be up to Congress to make up the difference.

Now one may ask what are the chances of Congress passing such legislation, and for the sitting president to sign the bill into law. Fair question.

Congress, it should be noted, is not loath to provide for raises. Some of the approval for such monetary enhancements has happened at late night sessions. This measure as well might conceivably be tacked on to other bills as a rider.

There's little doubt that politicians of all stripes, and at all levels, would appreciate the insurance such a measure provides.

Let's be kind to fallen politicians, especially if they show remorse and welcome rehabilitation.

2 – Gridlock Video

Let's play "Gridlock!"

We should all hail a new video game under development. It eschews violence and gore and instead provides interesting and informative background on current political issues in an exciting and dramatic fashion. This isn't to say that politics isn't also a blood sport but Gridlock doesn't feature any severed limbs, perforated bodies, or the squirting of torrents of ersatz blood. Diminished egos as well as faulty political campaigns and legislative struggles are more likely.

This new video pastime is probably destined to catch on with a larger segment of the adult public than the usual number of youthful players, who would still constitute a major market. While appealing to players of all age, Gridlock would serve as a potentially useful if whimsical game to stimulate interest in our larger and more significant game of national politics. Voting rolls are likely to expand.

Gridlock, as its name suggests, pits Republics and Democrats sitting in a large chamber as it might be with the president's State of the Union address. Only here the president is not shown. A bill on a particular issue is then projected on the screen. It could be on any of the pressing subjects confronting Congress and the nation – gun controls, immigration, lowering the debt, budgetary considerations, entitlements such as Social Security and Medicare, etc.

This is where the fun begins. One "champion" from each party rises and comes to the foreground. Players can press a button to pick a champion from each party but there wouldn't be any recognizable names or faces other than the party designation. The control area would have a battery of "argument buttons" that cite major positions of each party. The champions, in effect would engage in non-lethal combat, using words and arguments that they fling at each other rather than guns or swords. Clearly, this would be much more civilized than the usual savagery of lethal video games.

The words, however, can be strong, accusatory, demagogic, vitriolic, mirroring in some way real-life commentary that might not get into the Congressional Record in a real political setting but are quite employable in a video game. No verbal holes barred, but with limits to be determined on curse words. Nothing worse, though, than what is aired on prime time television today. Players can also press a button to show a facial expression. Mocking. disdainful, approving and uncertain looks would be the primary options. The player choosing the Democrat side would pick the reaction for his Republican opponent and vice versa.

A numerical value would be given to each exchange between the champions. After a set number of exchanges, with this amount still to be determined, a final score would be shown along with the verdict of pass or fail for the relevant bill.

More nuances and enhancements are likely to be added to the first generation of Gridlock. Many observers of the cultural scene are already applauding advent of a more peaceful video game, though some voice fears that game manufacturers are weaving in political messages that favor liberal or more conservative values. Manufacturers, on the other hand, are welcoming conspiracy theories as marketing tools.

Some game enthusiasts even venture that Gridlock will enter future history books as another marker of the so-called "culture" war.

But in the more immediate analysis Gridlock, once put into commercial production, seems virtually certain to make Congress and the overall political scene more understood than ever before. The educational benefits are clear. On a social scale, it might even lessen any generational gap, with more adults playing the game with their children.

Gridlock, overcoming any negativity to its name, could prove to be a winner on many fronts.

3 – New Generation Of Military Names

New aircraft destroyers, cruisers, battleships and other ships in our vast fleet usually are named after esteemed political leaders and other famous personalities. But many feel the time has come to apply the names of current issues to celebrate the advent of new fighting vessels.

Such names should show or commemorate the fight over problems that have confronted and bedeviled the nation.

Accordingly, new ships of any size or shape could be named the S.S. Fiscal Cliff, S.S. Entitlements, and even S.S. Spending. Other names that have come under consideration include S.S. Medicare and S.S. Social Security. Both of the latter two names were deemed worthy as servicemen and women would surely have use of both programs later in life. Opponents, however, argue that these names might be too disrespectful to the issues and the political process in which they are discussed. Some observers also feel such names are too pedestrian and non-nautical, and might even stir political discord and passions that could roil a ship's crew, both officers and enlisted personnel.

Such a departure in naming ships, however, would have several benefits.

Names like these would serve as lasting reminders of the political turmoil in Washington D.C. about the country's financial situation. Officers and crews alike would realize even more clearly than before in what light they were protecting and fighting the nation's battles. Such insights could only bolster their pride and spirits in tense moments of action. Regardless of any prior political opinions, these names of fighting vessels would serve as a uniting factor in facing the country's foes.

In fact, the salutary impact of these names among our fighting men and women would bring about greater cohesion in successfully undertaking a military purpose or mission. While it may seem ironic, such names could be a model to foster a more comradely atmosphere in the nation's capital for our ongoing struggle to defeat our adversaries. The military, though, would certainly remain subservient to our civilian leaders.

Moreover, the names would serve as sobering reminders of the huge cost of these ships and under what friction, considering the size of military budgets, that they might finally have been built. The bridge between our military and civilian sectors would be immensely strengthened. Moreover, the names would justly provide an enduring presence to our robust if sometimes untidy democratic values; the U.S. though, it should be noted and often isn't, is a republic and not a democracy.

This aspect, noting the sometimes caustic scenario in Congress affecting military budgets, can be enhanced aboard ship by special classes or workshops that go into the sundry background factors that caused initial division over reconciling cuts in spending and entitlements. These sessions would have to be conducted on a strict non-partisan basis, itself a signal victory for compromise and common sense. Conceivably, the military would serve as a role model in this sense to our constantly divisive political leaders.

Separate classes, if needed, could be given to officers and non-officers. However, the thought is that attendance would be mandatory from admiral or captain down to the lowest rank. Given the gravity and complexity of the subjects, several sessions may be needed.

The length and number of classes can be left to the ship's commander. In no way should such classes interfere with the regular duties of anyone aboard ship. Battle readiness remains the priority.

On the other hand, there is considerable support to employ special inspector generals who might show up at any time, aboard ship or while it's in port, to question officers and crew on their knowledge of such key subjects. If the ship gets a bad mark, that could damage the commander's record. Concern over military records, affecting promotions, usually serves as an excellent incentive to run things well.

More names have been tossed around. Some observers have even tended the names of "Compromise" and "Common Sense" for new ships. The name "Gridlock", however, was soundly defeated as much too negative. Somehow S.S. Gridlock just didn't have the right ring to it.

4 - Humor Calculator

It's probably only in the U.S. that prominent people, starting with the president, can be broadly lampooned. TV comedians feast on whatever tidbits they can hit upon. Viewers are likely unaware of the fierce drive by comedians, and their staff of writers, to create one-liners that can draw a quick laugh or smile.

This sort of pressure to produce laughs often leads entertainers to take considerable chances on material. Besides risking simply not being very funny, comedians can be roundly criticized for going too far and crossing the line into bad taste.

But there is no sure-fire indicator of what passes muster as reasonable humor. What tickles one person's funny bone can offend another. Being offensive obviously doesn't automatically equate to humor, broad-based or subtle.

The 2013 Academy Awards show provides a representative example. One joke was about Abraham Lincoln and the fatal bullet to hit his brain. Lincoln was certainly topical as a movie with the same name was up for various awards. But the one-liner seemed to fall flat judging from a brief sweeping view of the audience's reaction on the television screen. And there's no way one could tell how the vast number of viewers in the U.S. and around the world reacted. How many thought the sally was amusing? How many thought it was disrespectful and even inane?

Similarly, a skit by a presenter, Mark Wahlberg, utilized the teddy bear character from his popular movie, *Ted*. The cinematic "teddy bear" was characterized by having a foul mouth and making outrageous statements, which doubtless captivated many with the irreverent humor while some lines might have been deplored by others. In the skit, "Ted" delivered cracks about Jews running things in Hollywood. Some observers thought the "humor" anti-Semitic.

This small group of comments didn't seem to go over well either with the audience, but this estimate naturally has to be based on a quick view of the audience shown on the television screen. What's going on in households is another matter.

Movie and television trends have clearly been to allow more and more realistic language using curse words and scatological terms. Anatomical liberation has followed suit to some extent. Industry and governmental codes, such as exist, are tested consistently to see what barriers can be surmounted.

Given this armada of potentially offensive words and lines, what's a poor (not financially) comedian or television/movie writer/producer to do?

Never doubt American ingenuity. The calculator is a great invention and it has been put to many uses. People can use calculators, often available on web sites, to get information on foreign money exchanges, to estimate real estate matters, seek a credit score, and sundry other concerns.

The thought then is to devise a calculator, or even two related ones, which can help both entertainers and their audiences at home reach a reasonable conclusion in what might work as humor and what might not. Clearly, this type of calculator doesn't lend itself to special numerical measurements. Setting up the parameters would be tricky. The criteria would have to be radically different and be subject itself to different opinions.

The broad lines under consideration to date have three basic markers: reasonably humorous, borderline humorous, and in poor taste. Doubtless, sub-categories will emerge. Possibly various colors, following the pattern of traffic lights, might be applied, with green for humorous, yellow for border line, and red for crossing the line.

Entertainers might get an advance indication of proposed humor gained through a trial or focus group with this raw material then fed into the calculator. Similarly, another version might be developed whereby the public could feed suspect one- liners into a calculator for a quick evaluation. Surveys might even be employed to track public responses.

This may be an idea whose time has come.

5 - Bring Back The Whigs

Some pundits feel the Republican and Democratic political parties hold essentially the same policies as far as basic governmental and economic values. Both believe in our republican form of government and capitalism. Others charge, citing gridlock in Congress, that the two parties are hopelessly partisan and have an alarming difficulty in agreeing on many subjects.

It's also been noted that the advent of the Tea Party, hard-core no-tax conservatives who also espouse restrictive cultural values, has transformed the Republican party into a neo-conservative bastion. The Republican Party is no longer, and hasn't been for a while, a group with balanced viewpoints and ready to compromise on them with the Democrats. While it's trying to attract more people of color and Hispanics, many moderates have left the party, either driven out at the ballot box, or simply resigning in disgust over the gridlock and its impact on the country.

Chances have been low of a third party ever making a breakthrough and amassing enough supporters to make it a credible choice in national elections. While a number of third parties have influenced elections – Ross Perot and Ralph Nader led parties certainly impacted recent presidential elections – they had no chance of actually winning. The U.S., for better or worse, seemed locked into a two-party system.

But now an opportunity may have risen with a new Whig Party possibly entering the political arena.

A quick review of history shows that the first Whig Party was active in the 1830-1855 period. Their members emerged from the Federalist Party, which faded away in the first decades of the 19th century, and various political dissidents. A common theme from Whig members was opposition to what they termed political and economic oppression. Two of its presidential candidates – William Henry Harrison and General Zachary Taylor - were elected president. Both died in office with Taylor succeeded by Millard Fillmore, another Whig stalwart. Fillmore, our 13th president, was the last Whig president. Abraham Lincoln, at one point, was a Whig leader in frontier Illinois.

An American or Know Nothing Party also came into existence during the latter part of this period.

The political demise of the Whig Party came about due to the epochal question of the expansion of slavery. The anti-slavery faction denied Fillmore renomination for a second term as president and instead nominated another general, Winfield Scott. Many Whigs promptly left politics or the party; some also changed parties, such as to the Know Nothings, or sought another outlet. Voters in the northern states joined the nascent Republican Party which was very different in those days than its version today.

The Whigs weren't represented in the 1856 election, with the new Republican party fielding frontier hero, John Fremont; the Democrats, a diplomat James Buchanan; and the Know Nothings, none other than the former Whig president, Millard Fillmore.

The Democrats won; the Know-Nothings faded into obscurity; and the Republicans went on to rival the Democrats as one of our two major parties – and to win the 1860 election with Lincoln, a former Whig and now Republican, its standard bearer.

So the cycle of history should be carefully considered.

Let the Tea Party and their supporters leave the Republican Party and become the new Whig Party. The Republicans can return to the values that represented them for many years. It's possible that some Democrats, in this political changeover, could even opt to become Republicans once the party's platform broadened.

At the end of the shake-up the country would be all the stronger for three clear-cut parties.

As usual, there would be the customary cries of would-be patriots that we were following in the footsteps of European governments with a bewildering array of parties that lead to frequent political upheavals and instability. But this wouldn't at all be true. The U.S. would still have a vibrant and constitutional balance of powers between the executive, Congress, and the judiciary. We'd still have presidential elections every four years. There wouldn't be calls for new elections just because the party in office seemed to be out of favor over an issue or issues.

Achieving political clarity would be worth a period of some confusion – something we're used to anyhow - during the rebirth of an old party

6 - Public Pulpit/Limp Pulpit

After the president gives his State of the Union address, a spokesman for the other party gets an immediate opportunity to counter the president's speech and any claims about past accomplishments, the current pulse of the nation, and various proposals for the future.

Both sides have been heard from, though the opposing party has less time to state its case. But the public hasn't been given a chance to voice an opinion of these talks and issues during the same general time frame.

To provide an even greater balance a drive has arisen to offer a random member of the public a chance to express a view point on both the president's speech and the other party's comeback. This person's comments, coming last, would be expected to touch on both sides, though proportionally most of his or her points would be about the president's address.

Such a speaker has already been dubbed "Mr. Average Citizen." Several names have been given to this inchoate talk, some respectful such as the "Public Pulpit" and some less so like the "Limp Pulpit" as a counterpoint to the "Bully Pulpit" label. Proponents and critics of the idea both agree that use of the term "pulpit" is fitting. If the president has a bully pulpit, why not let the public have its pulpit too?

Those in favor of a "pulpit" reserved for a public representative claim the basic term works to encompass the people at large, and to be a shining if telegenic symbol of democracy in real time action.

Opponents deride the notion as a futile and meaningless attempt to throw a bone to the public. Not that many viewers stay tuned to hear the other party offer its rebuttal to the president's points and even fewer, they contend, would bother to listen to some unknown speaker expound on issues they might not fully understand.

Supporters of the proposal argue that regardless of the title accorded to this new potential talk, the key point remains that the public gets a timely crack at responding to the themes and claims served up by each party.

The talk by the public representative would also be considerably shorter than the president's speech and not as long as the rebuttal address by the opposing party.

Only someone who has a proven track record as an independent voter would be given the honor of speaking to the country on national television on such an auspicious occasion. This person's voting record would be carefully scrutinized, and he or she would be vetted in other ways too. In fact, it's suspected that some people might decline the honor to avoid intrusive scrutiny. Being in the public eye would doubtless bring considerable media attention, as well as local fame, and this position in the public eye isn't always welcome. On the other hand, many would probably covet the honor.

At this juncture, the expectation is that the public pulpit speaker would alternate between men and women. Citizens from all walks of life would be eligible. Selections would be made from states that aren't considered hard core "red" or "blue."

Television networks would, of course, have to agree to furnish free airtime to a public pulpit speaker. As the talk would be short, and doubtless preceded and followed by commercials, this factor isn't expected to be a problem.

There wouldn't be much pre-screening of what the public speaker might say other than to receive assurances that his or her talk would obey normal courtesies. This person would have a private perch to watch both the president's address and the follow-up by the other party. This would allow the person to take notes and jot down thoughts which would be harder to do if sitting in the audience for the president's address.

Both parties, naturally, would have to agree to this proposal. Neither side is expected to turn the idea down in fear that it would be used against them in future campaigns.

In the Obama-McCain campaign, Joe the Plumber surfaced. Who knows what other colorful personalities may come to address the nation, even perhaps upstaging both political parties?

7 – Catch 22 Concentrate

The phrase "Catch 22" has become part of everyday vocabulary in signifying a situation where a sensible solution is impossible because of illogical rules or conditions which often are tricky, senseless, and unfair.

Every so often a catch-22 situation emerges as our governing bodies do their official duties, and the importance of these moment is often downplayed or simply ignored by media. The public at large remains largely ignorant. Even if there is some initial awareness, the news value is limited and soon evaporates under the relentless pressure of the 24/7 news cycle.

One of the more recent examples came with a Supreme Court decision on the government's electronic surveillance program. A group of intrepid journalists, activists and attorneys filed a suit claiming that a 2008 law that authorized the electronic surveillance of non-Americans abroad violated the constitutional rights of Americans whose phone conversations and email messages might be ensnared as well. The surveillance, of course, is done on a highly secretive basis.

The case wound up before the Supreme Court which voted in another dread five to four decision - with the conservative quintet winning out - to dismiss the case without hearing pro and con arguments. The labored reasoning of the majority of justices boiled down to the grounds that the plaintiffs didn't even have the right – in legal parlance, the standing or concrete interest in a legal dispute – to sue in the first place because they lacked specific proof that their conversations/messages had been included in the customary sweeps.

This is the catch-22 part. How can the plaintiffs prove their calls/messages had been intercepted, overheard and assessed by government security personnel unless they could gain sufficient access to the overall roster of international phone and email messages? As the furtive program currently stands – it was recently extended - the government doesn't have to provide any accounting of its surveillance operations.

Few would argue that the government shouldn't expend every legitimate effort to combat terrorism. We are fighting an asymmetric war against terrorist groups and the struggle inevitably calls for some lamentable but necessary impositions on the public. But the counter consideration is that a balance has to be established between needed security measures and precautions and the need to avoid disrupting the fabric of a free society in this way. Preservation of the right to some elemental privacy in electronic communications is a subject that deserves more of a judicial airing. If we lose too much of our basic freedom – what we're fighting for – the terrorists gain a victory.

In these days the number of true believers that the government is always wise in its decisions and actions has decreased by a wide margin. Death pangs for this belief by the American public began with the Watergate debacle and have only increased since. Since the prevailing sentiment denies infallibility to the government, it seems to follow that more accountability should be directed at secretive operations.

At the very least the subject should be heard by our highest court, and their reluctance to do so should get a bigger splash in media.

Accordingly, there is growing interest in creating a catch-22 web site, more than just a blog, which would be limited to catch-22 situations in governmental operations, and covering the span from municipal to federal.

People could cite what they believe to be specific catch-22 situations, and everyone else could register their opinions on the specific issues involved. It's thought that the number of posts would quickly mount. Hopefully, government officials would take note. Possibly some injustices might be remedied and questionable policies either reexamined or reversed.

Who knows, the Supreme Court might rule too on important cases – one way or another – that is, if such cases were actually debated by the justices.

8 - Apps Away

Living in the age of information has its benefits and perils.

On the plus side we're better informed or we can be. We can make better use of the vast reservoir of information indiscriminately poured forth through an increasing number of channels, stations, web sites, and other outlets. Or we can just accept what we deem useful and discard the rest, though this is increasingly difficult. Another option, and a rather popular one, is to numbly ignore virtually the entire storehouse of information paraded in front of us, ignoring gems as well as dross.

This pattern of essentially giving-up in this battle of informational overkill has dangerous drawbacks that can weaken the national character.

The full flood of technological advances is seemingly growing faster than our capacity to absorb the characteristics of each device and its apps or applications. The word "apps" itself is another abbreviation to stow away in our overcrowded minds.

Consequently, a number of thoughtful savants, technically gifted by endowment but also blessed with caring souls, are working on a new app that will permit users to know when they've reached an overload of information. The concept is quite simple. Your mind is treated, with no slur intended, as a load of laundry in the wash. If there's too much laundry thrown in, the wash machine doesn't work. So it goes with our mental facilities.

In the device being worked on, one will be able to use relevant buttons on the app to calculate, using some input, to place yourself on a scale of mind storage. In a sense it's like using a calculator to figure out a mortgage or currency exchange. Input levels might need to be finessed to offer a range of informational cut-off points. Decisions still have to be made if there should be buttons based on words or concepts.

The advantages, once every aspect is fine-tuned, will be enormous. People can quickly free their minds of excess information that strangles what they do need to know. They'll realize when to stop the onslaught of information that may have little relevance to their lives and activities. Lives will be simpler though the times get more complex. A pervasive sense of understated bewilderment, more universal than generally recognized, will be blunted if not erased. Because the confusion is so commonplace, people tend to shrug it off. But with this new app their self-realization will be meaningfully sharpened.

The significance of this app will be felt in virtually every sphere of activity, but perhaps no more dramatically than in the world of politics. Considering the spew of exaggerations, half-truths, and sheer lies that emanate from ostensible leaders, such a greater command will enable people to make wiser decisions on their choices of who to support and who to vote for.

Moreover, with the advent of such an app, politicians will be forced to take note and clean up their acts.

In the medical field, sessions with doctors and dentists will be enriched by patients enabled to express clearer questions and to extract clearer answers. Any legal situation, especially involving lawyers, will be greatly clarified. The same would go for any dealings with insurance companies, health medical organizations, and any entity that might currently befuddle people with their spoken and written declarations. The latter missives are often evasive and intentionally muddled with blatant examples of legalese.

Socially, relationships will be more focused. Accuracy, if not truth, will be more paramount. Divorces may become less frequent as couples will be less surprised at what their spouses know and think. Along with the strengthening of marriages, the rearing of children will be enhanced by what parents need to know. Their progeny will mature with a more secure grasp on the world they face. Everyone will find a measure of individual satisfaction in both a brave and better- controlled informational world.

Apps away!

9 - It's Jobs, Stupid!

Doing something for the unemployed has taken on more and more urgency as a national problem and as an aid to diminish the pains of the affected.

Providing more weeks of benefits is impeded by budgetary difficulties and tied to bitter debates between the Republicans and Democrats on working down the deficit. Hope is limited on that score.

Some thought has been given to providing IOU's for when the economy is in better shape and the national debt has been reduced. Circumstances suggest that this belated benefit would most likely have to be made retroactive for the heirs of the unemployed.

Many people who are unemployed have already been assisted on the educational front to learn new skills to meet the needs of a changing employment scene due to technological advances and corporate contractions.

Now, mindful of the suffering experienced by the unemployed, some thoughtful observers have come up with a proposal to provide them with another benefit. This benefit, however, wouldn't be financial or educational; but hopefully it can help restore any loss of pride and desire to be involved with the public scene. The idea is to let the unemployed field their own political candidates on ballots for national elections. No one expects their candidates to actually win an election, though they could possibly siphon valuable votes from major Republican or Democrat candidates. Third parties of one stripe or another have significantly influenced prior elections.

Obviously, candidates who have favorable voting records on unemployment issues are going to fare better with this bloc of voters. Their sheer presence on ballots may help spur responsive legislation to ease the burden of people without jobs.

Proponents of this proposal assert that candidates put forward by the unemployed wouldn't have to come from a new party. Enough small parties now crowd ballots. Nor would the unemployed need to produce the requisite number of signatures, or other procedures necessary to establish a bona fide political party.

Congress, under this plan, would simply grant the unemployed in every congressional district the right to present their own candidate in federal elections. A representative of the unemployed would be on the ballot for presidents, senators, and members of the House of Representatives.

While some might deride this program as a shallow and meaningless gesture, it's felt by many that it would be a profound note of reassurance that the nation cares for the plight of the jobless.

The cost of such a program on a federal basis would be quite minimal. Nor would the tab set back the shrunken wallets of the unemployed who could choose their candidates through several inexpensive ways, with the Internet the best bet. Those eligible to vote can make a choice online from a roster of candidates assembled by suggestions. The five to ten candidates with the most online votes would then have a run-off online.

At this juncture someone would have to be unemployed for at last 26 weeks to qualify to vote.

On the negative side, it's also recognized that voting on the "unemployed ticket" could prevent someone from voting from a candidate who could actually win. Making their voice heard, proponents contend, would be a stronger factor. However, it's expected that a provision will be created whereby someone could vote for the "unemployed" candidate and still make a second choice.

While the "unemployed" votes would be tallied, it wouldn't affect the outcome other that symbolically. This measure would open the election up to everyone not just those looking for work, but that isn't considered a bad development at all. Voters could vote for their preferred candidate and still make a statement about the employment scene.

The party name on the ballot could just be "Unemployed." A special committee of the unemployed is currently developing other parts of the inchoate program. A national search is being made for a suitable slogan. At this time the favorite is "It's jobs, stupid!"

10 - Latter-day Humiliation

Many Americans chafe at how well-heeled financial executives at Wall Street finance and investment firms talent managed to escape any charges of criminal or civil misconduct in the aftermath of the recent financial scandals, let alone jail terms for their misdeeds which plunged the country and the world itself into a downward economic spiral. Top-level legal talent, charging shocking hourly fees, probably earned their retainers and fees.

The financial firms, with one exception, were considered too big to fail. This didn't necessarily mean that these executives were too big to suffer the consequences of their bungling, but that's how it mostly worked out. Their actions or inactions were clearly wrong, but it was felt, logically enough, that it was more important to save our financial structure than to exact legal consequences to the involved executives. It wasn't a matter of plea bargaining or anything of that sort. They were just off the hook, enjoying large bonuses and subsequently dispensing equally large bonuses to some of the people who caused the financial upheavals in the first place.

Justice was obviously thwarted in some cases. Some financial personalities, such as Bernie Medoff, have been brought to justice. But many culprits avoided much more than a semblance of stigma and have gone on to enjoy their second homes, yachts, and like elements of the good life.

A possible way to bring about some modicum of basic fairness has been bruited by citizens concerned that such injustice lets the wrong-doers get away, and even profit from their malfeasance. Moreover, the disquieting fall-outs provide a sorry model to the nation's youth.

One proposal getting serious consideration is applying a form of televised humiliation. As legal recourse and financial penalties are gone as effective means of achieving commensurate justice, an old instrument may be brought back. The pillory was in use in bygone days, mostly in the colonial period. A person's head and hands were placed in holes in the wooden device. The pillory was placed in public places where the townspeople could see them and jeer the imprisoned and often throw rotten fruit and other non-lethal items at them.

Some elements of latter-day stockades would resurface. Under one scenario envisioned, such financial executives who escaped harsher consequences would be compelled to being put into a pillory for at last thirty seconds during prime time on television. A simple announcement could be made just stating the name and title of the person in the pillory and the relevant charge. The same information could appear at the bottom of the screen. The amount of time that these spots, which are really public service announcements in a sense, would vary according to the severity of the past scandals.

The person in the pillory would also have to pay for the television spots, adding to the humiliation.

Concern has, of course, come over whether such treatment violates someone's constitutional rights over not being subject to cruel and unusual punishments. This aspect would probably come down to a Supreme Court decision.

Being in a pillory is certainly unusual in the modern age, but pillories don't inflict physical pain. Discomfort surely, but with such a limited amount of time involved, that factor is minimal. The cruelty element is debatable. What's cruel to one person might not be to another. No one would be tossing insults or physical items at them. Nor would they be out in the open subject to cold, heat, rain or snow or objects thrown at them. At the very least, media coverage of the proposal itself might serve as a warning to other financial miscreants of the punishment they might face.

Meanwhile, the idea has led some companies to put more modern pillories on their drawing boards. Some manufacturers might even have the wooden surfaces coated with softer fabrics. As a further concession to those who might find themselves subject to such a procedure, they would be allowed to choose the color scheme of the pillory they'd be seen in on television.

Fair is fair.

11 - Baseball Drug League

As more and more stories surface about professional baseball ballplayers who have used drugs to enhance their careers, even greater disillusionment has set in with fans and non-fans. Widespread belief exists that what is known, or suspected, is just the tip of a huge iceberg that might sink Major League baseball.

The decision by the Baseball Hall of Fame to deny admission to some big name players such as Barry Bonds, Roger Clemens, and Sammy Sosa clearly indicates that sports writers who vote think records of players who use drugs to amass their records shouldn't be compared to those who did. Statistics are an important aspect of baseball and many want their sanctity protected.

The tests applied to weed out users seem on the weak side, just levying a fifty game suspension for the first offence, one hundred games for the second offence, and a ban from Major League baseball for a third offence. Moreover, tests may be inconclusive, or somehow be tainted in handling.

The debacle involving Lance Armstrong, in another sport, gave the overall anti-doping impetus even more impetus.

There may be a way to salvage baseball.

To start, Major League baseball was once just one league. Then, in the early part of the 20th century, it split into National and American Leagues as the number of teams increased. Now it's time for another even more drastic split, not to accommodate more teams but to separate drug-users from other players.

Under this set-up, players known to be using, or have used drugs, would just play in their own league. Players in the major leagues, and minor leagues as well, would be given an option in which league to play. A blanket amnesty would be given for any current or prior drug use. But if a player who decided to stay in the non-drug leagues, the traditional Major Leagues and Minor League system, were found to be using drugs, he would be banished from professional baseball in any league for life. This might seem harsh, but trust in such a system has to be earned. Players would be reluctant to risk such an end to their career by lying and then be caught. It would be better, they would surely realize, to just switch to the new drug league.

Stocking teams with "drug" players might seem difficult at first. The number of teams, with the same current roster allocation of twenty-five players, would have to be built up from scratch. Initially, and for a number of years, there would probably just be one league with a limited number of teams. However, giving the known and suspected roster of drug users, the number of teams would doubtless increase. Baseball, still the national sport, will continue to lure many hopeful youths to its fold.

It should be noted that new drugs are likely to come into existence and possibly be harder to detect.

Another factor which many players who toiled and now play in the Minor Leagues would appreciate is a quicker rise to "The Show" – the Major Leagues. Minor league players would be called up to replace players on major league teams going over to the drug league, and to man new teams. Quicker rise would translate into higher salaries. As it is, Major League ballplayers are often paid astronomical sums. Players in the Drug League would soon get to have their own union, with the precedent of how effective the union for Major League players has been on their collective behalf.

Consequently, records – symbols of achievement to fans as well as owners paying awesome salaries - would be kept separately by each league..

Many other key questions would be answered in time. Would teams in the drug league have their own World Series? Their own Hall of Fame, which others might dub the Hall of Shame? Would they ever meet non-drug teams in games? Would every city accept a drug team? Would such drug teams attract and sustain fan loyalty? Would television networks and radio stations cover drug games? Would marketing opportunities to sell helmets, caps and other items be limited? What about billboards, brochures, and ads? Baseball has grown in popularity in other countries. How would an American drug league affect the international scene?

Many questions arise, and more study is obviously likely to take place. But the seed may have been planted.

New enterprises may start slowly, but this one would be born out of necessity. It should protect the purity of Major League baseball and remove now and for the future any suspicions about players bulking up through drug use.

A small price to play.

12 - Revisionism, American Style

Revisionism can be a national pastime, and there is concern that the U.S. not fall victim to this insidious practice.

Every nation has probably been responsible for acts of commission and omission in its past that are questionable if not clearly wrong. How a country handles elements of its history it would rather be forgotten, distorted, or ignored is another matter. Some nations go farther and challenge the accuracy of events.

Turkey, for example, has long disputed its massacre of Armenians in 1915, though the slaughter is widely considered to be the first holocaust of the 20th century.

A Japanese prime minister has alleged, against convincing evidence otherwise, that it never forced foreign women into sexual slavery at its Army-run brothels during World War II. A former Italian prime minister has whitewashed Benito Mussolini – the country's World War II dictator – for his collaboration with Hitler and Nazi Germany.

Doubtless there are other example as well.

Even nations not directly responsible for heinous acts can dispute that they ever took place. Witness the claims by the head of the Iranian government denying that the World War II holocaust of European Jews ever occurred.

To some, such pretences, while officially sanctioned, are proof that the bigger the lie the more people may believe it. Geopolitical and economic issues come into play, and truthfulness is often sacrificed to not offend allies and to maintain what passes for world order.

Even if disbelief exists, weariness sets in and an armistice of sorts comes into being on a vast scale. Textbooks may be created or revised to promulgate badly flawed versions of history. False notions are fed into young minds.

The U.S. hasn't been guilty of such arrant revisionism though there are incidents in our history that are far from commendable. However, text books in some states – Texas is one – have shone an uncertain light on some aspects of our history. A distorted sense of patriotism may overcome accuracy. On the other hand, we have belatedly apologized for some incidents such as internment of Americans of Japanese descent into modified concentration camps during World War II. Some apologies have been made for the relentless absorption of Indian lands and broken treaties with various tribes during our advancing frontier days. No apology, however, has been made for the less than pure efforts made to successfully take over virtually one-third of Mexico in the mid 19th century. Nor has any apology been forwarded – or expected – for our obvious support of right wing dictators around the world, or in our part in helping locals stage revolutions and upheavals such as took place in Iran, Chile and Guatemala.

The notion of American Exceptionalism is thrust forward as if this self-anointment automatically voids any possibility of national mischief. The U.S. is a remarkable nation, and very much a model and beacon to the rest of the world, for its democratic values and culture. But we're not perfect, far from it.

Now there is consideration, by volunteers, of forming a National Revisionism Council to be composed of volunteers drawn from historians and college professors. Ironically, the purpose of the council would be to forestall any revisionism. Its mandate would be to sift through every aspect of our history and determine if any acts – again commission and omission – need to be revisited and perhaps more honestly considered than previously. Chances are many incidents would be found.

Subsequently, the committee would issue recommendations as to what level of latter-day accountability is called for. Their findings, which would be published in due course, wouldn't be binding. But it's hoped that whatever administration is in office will pay proper heed. Educators and textbook publishers should also follow recommendations. Teachers could make good use of the findings in classrooms across the country.

No state should be allowed to dictate, or have published, contrary declarations about American history.

This would be revisionism, American style.

13 - Political Privatization

"Political privatization" may become a reality in the U.S. if certain business and political interests get their way. The way we are governed may be better or worse, but it will certainly be different.

A truly radical study of governance in the U.S. is being contemplated.

The business community, backed for the most part by the Republican Party, have long maintained that the private sector is far more efficient and better suited to run many federal operations than the governmental agencies themselves.

Now the concept may be put to a final test.

This study involves placing one major government agency completely under the aegis of a private company. The Department of the Interior has been chosen for a comprehensive study. The current head of the department will serve as a consultant, and have the power of veto. The policies of the agency, as directed by the president, would still be in effect but their administration would be handled by the private company.

The initial statistical analysis meant that a significant part of the agency's work force wouldn't be needed. However, no one would lose their job, with most staffers no longer needed transferred to other governmental agencies.

Proponents of such turnovers contend that besides the savings in salaries, the analysis also showed a considerable dent in a budget for the agency even after the sum provided to the private company for its work. Sharper administration practices and reduction of redundant work would bring about an overhaul in efficiency. Secret bids would be taken for this responsibility, with the lowest bid accepted. However, the amount to be paid to the private outfit has still not been settled. But all savings would be used to lessen the national deficit. Congressional oversight would still be applied, but it's anticipated that Congress would accept any reasonable budget.

If the experiment were actually implemented, it would be for a one-year period to allow sufficient time for a separate study by the government on each facet of the program. The public would be advised of each step in the process.

Supporters of the changeover have already predicted that if the experiment is as successful as expected, the program will be expanded. There is no plan, of course, to ever turn the entire federal government over to private companies for operation. One thought is to utilize this system on a rotating basis, but this method has been criticized for leading to a loss of continuity in administration.

At this point, only federal agencies dealing with domestic matters are likely to fall under a possible mix of those agencies and departments subject to being run by the private sector. Foreign affairs are considered too complex and complicated for this program, and there is concern that other nations might look askance at the notion of their dealing with business personnel rather than our normal leaders.

Concerns have been voiced over the possibility of private interests working, directly or indirectly, to benefit the business sector. The interests of the public, they argue, might often turn out to be a second priority when it comes to such matters as environmental matters, protecting American companies and their employees, and a roster of other outstanding issues.

However, some observers have contended that the private sector could hardly do worse than what the Department of Labor. Federal Trade Commission, and other potential candidates for this program have done -- or not done. Moreover, an additional plan is being considered whereby the U.S., possibly with the cooperation of the United Nations, will seek to export the system to developing countries for their internal use.

Under no circumstances, though, would American companies be allowed to serve in such private, non-governmental capacities. As one proponent put, "We certainly don't want to seem like a super-power in the private sector as well. Being a role model is enough."

14 - Quarter The Veterans

The Bill of Rights prohibits the quartering of soldiers in private homes during peacetime without the consent of the owner, and only in wartime as prescribed by law. As many argue, we're now in a period of asymmetric warfare and there is no peace; in addition, the government has already shown it can kill American citizens abroad considered guilty of terrorism without any legal niceties. But there's no likelihood of the government forcing citizens to host soldiers in their homes.

Moreover, there's nothing to forbid voluntary stays by returning veterans to spend a limited amount of time in the homes of ordinary American citizens.

The advantages of such a program could be enormous. The veterans would likely feel more appreciated and have a much easier time returning to civilian life. There would, hopefully, be much less of the resentment that many veterans of the Viet Nam War felt upon their return. Similarly, veterans who came back from the two Iraq wars, and those already returned from the conflict in Afghanistan, would doubtless be grateful for a more thoughtful welcome.

Clearly, not all of our recent wars have been resounding successes, though our armed forces have performed with great heroism and have suffered many sacrifices.

In this fashion, veterans - in some cases but not all - could have a useful transitional period. One month has been suggested as the optimal period, though this could be shortened or lengthened as the partners decide. It's felt that it might be preferable to lodge veterans in a different community than there whey come from. Such an arrangement might mean less interference or disruption of any kind through family and/or communal dynamics. But it's recognized that sometimes it might be preferable to have home comforts. Each case would have to be decided on its own merits and obviously on a subjective basis. Trained counselors can be expected to make wise decisions.

Whether it would be easier or harder for veterans to discuss their war experiences with people, who were initial strangers, is unknown. In some cases it might be easier; in others, more difficult. Chances are, however, that a great deal of truthful material would be disclosed that might never be known otherwise.

The American people would learn, as never before, the true nature of our military involvements abroad which covers much more than actual combats. We have military forces, of one kind or another, stationed around the world. Intelligence operations, drone stations, security at embassies, and a bunch of other duties are scattered in many nations. There are well over 700 bases or installations involving more than two million American personnel. The scope and extent of our forces positioned internationally would receive more national attention than ever before. A more enlightened public would be able to assess our political and military posture with greater acuity.

The geography lessons themselves would be extraordinary, putting the location of places like Djibouti, Diego Garcia, Bahrain, Tajikistan and other exotically named spots in Africa, the Persian Gulf, and Central Asia more in the public's mind.

The program would be entirely voluntary for both hosts and veterans. Moreover, there would be no expense to the government. If a veteran needed any health or other services provided by the Veteran's Administration, they could still go to the nearest VA office. The host family would probably provide transportation in many situations. The VA, of course, would be notified if any major problem ensued and be responsible for appropriate action. Veterans, unfortunately, do suffer from various traumatic disorders after discharge and the suicide rate has been sadly high.

The publicity that could emanate from this program might actually work against it. Accordingly, little fanfare would be given to it. Some families might welcome inquiring reporters; other would view it as an invasion of their privacy. This factor would obviously come into play in making the decision on whether to participate or not. Local media, no doubt, would soon learn of such unexpected veterans in their midst and possibly seek interviews.

Veterans would be interviewed first before discharge to determine their interest. The military, in coordination with the social services office of cities, would interview prospective families who might be interested in the program. Putting the two together would follow. Either party would be able to end the arrangement at any time.

Give the program a shot.

15 - Vote/Dine/Shop

Another way has been devised to possibly improve the means by which people can exercise their constitutional right and civic duty to vote in national elections. If the measure comes to pass, the social fabric – at least on one day – might become an entirely new ballgame. Dismal voting records would quickly be surpassed every four years, given the increase in the population.

The number of people voting in presidential elections is shockingly low, considering the importance of the election. While many bemoan this disgraceful non-performance by our citizenry, little is actually done to redress the sad situation.

A key way to generate more voters is to finally make Election Day a national holiday. But the powers-that-be still consider such a loss of a full day of work to be too costly to the economy. Another suggestion to move the day of voting from Tuesday to the nearest Saturday has never received much support. Likewise, the possibility of allowing voting for the entire weekend failed to garner much support since it would expand the operating hours of the voting centers and add to the overall costs.

Accordingly, other ways have been sought to accomplish the same purpose. One tactic under consideration is to develop the option of drive-through voting at major shopping malls. Americans, of course, already tend to spend a good amount of time in their cars, and such an enablement to vote would only add another merit of usefulness to their trusty vehicles.

Under this system, registered voters could stay in their cars while attending to their civic duty. Voters would simply drive up to special booths, have their names and addresses checked off, and then receive a voting ballot and special pen – all just as traditionally takes place in someone's garage, or a school or church room/hall. They could even munch away at hamburgers and drink sugar-laden sodas while expressing their decisions on candidates.

After casting their ballots, the voter would simply hand in their ballot and pencil and receive the usual tab as proof of having voted. The entire process wouldn't take any longer than when one stands and votes at a district voting center, and possibly it could be faster. The amount of time waiting in the car lane isn't expected to be excessive, though this element would have to be watched closely.

Another advantage to this system, as far as voters' lifestyles, is that they would be able to combine voting with quick dining. This in turn would make, hopefully, for a more productive workday. Voting would also seem to some as less of a chore and more of a pleasurable outing. If one wanted to shop as well as vote, they would already be in position. Conceivably, vendors in the mall could come up with various voting promotions and discounts that would also serve as a lure for voters to express their choices for who runs the country.

On the other hand, it would be forbidden for any material given to voters at the special booths such as napkins, wrappers, paper plates and straws to contain political messages of any sort.

In another wrinkle, standard voting booths could be set up in malls (and possibly even at department stores). Dining and shopping could also be features of the overall experience. The cost to install the special voting booths, which would be run by volunteers just as takes place in regular voting areas, would be minimal. Only a few volunteers would be needed at any of these locations.

Conceivably, a move might be made to get the malls to bear the expense of creating the new facet as the influx of voters would surely lead to more food and merchandise being sold. It probably wouldn't take long for the malls to recoup their investments. Similarly, voting at high traffic points at a department store might lead to more sales, at least on that floor.

Economists, however, are still studying the issue and the monetary consequences.

By and large, however, the prevailing thought about shopping mall voting booths is that what's good for the economy can also be good for the electoral process.

16 – Entitlements In Person

It may seem odd to consider a new entitlement when the cost of current entitlements such as Medicare, Medicaid and Social Security are such crucial subjects of disagreement in Congress. But there may be a future entitlement that takes a page from a practice in bygone kingdoms.

In olden days some enlightened monarchs would grant their subjects a weekly or monthly time period, perhaps a half-day or full day, where they could state their grievances and seek justice or redress in person at court and directly before the king. The people welcomed this opportunity to personally speak to the ruler, though they might not always be happy with his decisions.

Application of this ancient program to today could provide a strong boost to public involvement in government. It could be used at many levels of government, from municipal to federal. Possibly it could first be tested by one mayor at one major city such as New York, Chicago, or Los Angeles.

Eventually, the program – if it worked as well as anticipated – would take place in Washington D.C. It's thought that taking a slice of the president's time, when there are so many major domestic and international issues, might be a drawback even if such sessions were limited to a half day. Others contend the president would probably be able to hear a good number of petitioners in a half day.

Frequency of such presidential audiences could be limited to one half day on a bi-weekly basis. Weekly might be too much of an incursion on the president's time while monthly might seem too much of a public relations move.

Another option could be for aggrieved citizens to have a chance to express their situations to either the House of Representatives or the Senate when either is in session. Parties would be able to address the entire body as if they were a member of the House or Senate. It's argued that petitioners could simply contact and/or visit their individual representative or senator. But others contend that a larger audience would reflect a greater sense of democracy in action. Moreover, many issues likely to come up could have national relevance beyond one person's problem. .

Some pre-screening of what people would discuss is considered quite necessary. Accordingly, people wishing to make such an appearance would have to submit the general nature of their issue or grievance to a special non-governmental committee who would review applications and make recommendations. Every effort would be made to produce a reasonable national distribution of petitioners, with no one state getting an unfair share of appearances.

All such Presidential and/or Congressional sessions would be conducted on a strictly bipartisan basis. Naturally, such appearances would be televised. Petitioners would be limited in how much time they could speak in presenting their case. They might conceivably be coached by a lawyer in advance but only they would appear before the president.

Unlike regal audiences in the dim past, where a monarch could direct immediate adjudication of some sort, these hearings would just offer constituents a chance to air their grievances. All they could hope for would be some action to be taken subsequently.

All material disclosed in this fashion would go into official archives and belong to the government. Citizens taking advantage of this program could still make other use of their petitions, but they would be discouraged from trying to profit from them on a commercial basis. But some collection of such grievances before highly placed officials is likely to get published.

As with other entitlements, the cost factor has to be considered. The only cost to government would be the amount of time taken away from leaders in handling their other responsibilities. Supporters of this entitlement venture that this time allotment wouldn't put a crimp in their performance.

Otherwise, people making such appearances would bear the cost of getting to the nation's capital and their accommodations and other related expenses. Having such moments of fame would probably spur many to make the journey. Conceivably, they would even be able to get community support to defray the personal budget factor.

Overall, faith in government – sorely tested in recent years – would receive a tremendous surge through a surprising continuity of history.

Jack Adler

17 - 24/7 News Syndrome

We're locked into a 24/7 news cycle providing a constant flow of what passes for fresh news from around the country and the world. The accumulation of information and analyses can be overwhelming. Moreover, with television the main medium involved, the complexity and significance of key news items is lost in the avalanche.

Another factor is the drive for graphic images on television that can limit more incisive commentary. Constraints on time allotments for individual news items is often skimpy and crimp adequate depth of reportage.

To counter this unrelenting trend, there's a program being developed to help people to become a 24/7 news-watching personality. The prevalent feeling is that it's time for people to catch up to the barrage of constant news reportage.

It's impossible, many feel, to turn back the clock on the outpouring of news, some of which is vital with many lesser items fleshing out news reports and shows. Therefore, it's incumbent on people to find a way to cope with this unyielding ingestion of news. The revolution of news coverage has to be met with a counter-revolution of news reception by viewers.

The measures under discussion would be totally up to the individual to use as desired. Some people might need a complete overhaul on how they watch news on television, while a more modest work-up might be sufficient for others.

One of the key elements is a starting or default point of alertness. Many people watch news at night when they might be a bit weary from the day's work. Or they watch at breakfast when they're rushing to some extent in getting ready to leave for work, appointments, or errands. Looking at news shows with any sort of numbness can be detrimental. It isn't feasible to suggest viewers consistently stand up while watching news, though many might at breakfast time or when cooking dinner. Most people probably sit in comfortable chairs or couches at night.

Accordingly, a bracing device that one can set to fit individual body contours is being developed. Such an exterior armature, easily put on and taken off, will help make viewers strike a more alert posture and thus help their attentiveness. Some observers have likened this device to being a sort of news-watching girdle, but the jury is still out on how popular and how effective such a unit would be.

Another less physical measure under consideration is to induce, if necessary, a strong amount of skepticism. One doesn't have to be a thorough cynic to evince a reasonable amount of doubt. Much of what is bruited on television screens as fact may turn out to be questionable. Opinions are just that, opinions, and pundits are far from infallible. *Caveat emptor* – "let the buyer beware" - applies to watching news as well.

Consequently, a series of exercises is being developed that includes visual aids. People can obtain reminders of recent scandals in inexpensive and easy-to-read letter-size sheets or posters. Such debacles would include Watergate, Iran-Contra, and similar events which have shaken and eroded American belief in their government. These posters, which can just be taken out and used at appropriate moments, can even be stand-up items that can be placed on tables by chairs and couches where people sit while watching news.

Another measure contemplated would come into play only when more than one person is watching the news. In such instances, watchers would back each other up and this can be done swiftly and silently by simply passing the poster around or flashing it.

However, for those who want even better ways to insure that they've been transformed into fully cognizant 24/7 news personalities, a catchword cry was sought. Many words, phrases were considered. Finally, the greatest wake-up call chosen was:

"It's The News, Stupid!"

18 - Political Awards Ceremony

Every element of the entertainment industry finds a way to celebrate itself with awards given to performers in its genre. Two of the most famous are the Academy Awards and Golden Globe ceremonies which both receive a great deal of media attention and large television audiences. But there are other shows of the same vintage.

A drive to initiate a comparable annual awards ceremony to celebrate those in the political arena is beginning to receive a groundswell of support, with a committee of volunteers charged with a preliminary study.

It's immediately recognized that such a program would have to be non-partisan. Accordingly, the Republican and Democratic parties would alternate years in choosing a host. The host, however, could crack jokes lampooning members of any political party or movement. The material would be mostly about those in Washington D.C. and covering each branch of the government – executive, congress, and the judiciary/Supreme Court. Governors, however, would be included. No one, in theory, would be spared. Every attempt would be made to insure that jokes weren't indecent or in bad taste, but it's realized that standards on what words can be used on television has been considerably liberalized in recent years.

Opponents of such a ceremony, and there are many from all quarters, argue that such an event would be demeaning and disrespectful to our political process and could give ammunition to terrorists. They also carp at the notion of such awards being celebratory as some categories might poke fun at contenders and the victor in any category.

Others contend that recognizing acts of courage and foolishness alike has merit. Bucking party agendas in key congressional votes takes guts. Noting such self-destructive statements about rape by two aspirants for Senate seats in the 2012 election is well worth recognition, and so is a presidential candidate alleging that nearly half the country would never vote for him. The fact that such actions have already received widespread media attention is another factor.

The awards dinner, both sides agree, wouldn't be competition against the "White House Correspondents Dinner" and the "Gridiron Dinner." Both much admired events are held annually in Washington D.C. Neither of these dinners set up specific awards for various deeds and misdeeds by politicians of all stripes. Nor are they televised, though highlights are often aired.

The timing of such a ceremony is a key factor. The prevailing thought is that the ceremony should be kept as distant from elections as possible. As we have national elections every two years, the window of opportunity isn't that great. Many prefer either March or April, after the state of the union speech and well before the following November.

The categories, of course, are the major topic of discussion. No final choices have been circulated for opinion. But it's agreed that there shouldn't be any breakdown by position. Everyone is in the mix.

To date, some of the positive awards would be given to the best political speech of the year, and most noteworthy act of political courage. There is some concern that not enough candidates can be found, but a thorough search will be conducted.

On the more flippant side, awards will be given for those who have raked in the most money through corporate donations, made the most foreign trips abroad at taxpayer expense, and made the biggest gaffes of the year. No one expects any difficulties on finding sufficient candidates for these awards.

An award, if enough candidates can be found, will go to the best political comeback of the year; and to those who made the most appearances on television news shows

No decision has been made as yet on who will vote, but the consensus is moving toward just using a small segment of media. A memorabilia segment of the program will be dedicated to any politician who had died.

Presenting these awards promises, if they come to pass, to be a highly entertaining show. Some of the awards, whether desired or not by recipients, may even wind up in later political campaigns.

19 - Making A Virtue of Political Families

There are manifold criticisms of how presidents are elected including the length and cost of campaigns. The recent decision by the Supreme Court allowing corporations, supposedly as people, to weigh in with their sizeable financial contributions, only worsened the problem.

While it may seem radical, there is a way to overcome this problem, at least for another forty years or so. We may look askance at other nations where the leader grooms his son to take over after him. Mubarak intended to do this in Egypt. Assad did it in Syria. But the people in these countries had little control over this sort of political ascension into power.

The plan for the U.S. is quite different.

Currently, we have two political families, the Clintons and the Bushes. Up to this point one of these families has been president for twenty years. Obama broke this run for two terms, but he won't be succeeded by anyone with the same family name. The Clintons and Bushes aren't dynasties by any stretch, but that's no reason why the presidency can't be kept between their families to give the U.S. a long and much needed respite from political strife.

In this scenario, Hillary Clinton could run for the presidency in 2016, win, and serve two terms. Subsequently, Jeb Bush could run in 2024 (if he's too old, another Bush could replace him), win, and serves two terms. Then, in 2032, Chelsea Clinton (who wouldn't be too old for the presidency) could take over the reins for two terms until 2040.

By that year the country would doubtless be tired of the Clinton and Bush names and be eager to see people with different names – as well as faces - vie for the presidency. Of course, there's no doubt either that many already are already surfeited with the Bush/Clinton personas.

But this aspect has to be measured against the extraordinary political stability the country would have for nearly half a century. The financial savings, and possible diminution of the federal debt, would be immense. The nomination aspect would be shorter, and campaigns might be, too. While it may seem trivial, the airwaves would be freer of incessant commercials extolling the virtues of one candidate and deficiencies of the other. Indeed, with the distressing proof that negative commercials work, the country might see a welcome change from the usual poisonous attacks.

This agreement between the Republican and Democrat parties would obviously be nonpartisan and beneficial to both sides. While there would be critics and opponents it's up to the parties who they nominate to run for president.

A cogent argument against this proposal, naturally, is that it takes away the possibility of other promising candidates coming to the fore in each party. This is a fair criticism, but the disservice to a generation or so of potentially worthy candidates also has to be weighed against the greater benefits of a type of political security this country has never had. Key figures would still arise and their voices would be heard. Their messages might even be stronger, given the American penchant to root for the underdog.

Historically, there have been other political families, though more divided in time while they served as president. These presidents include John Adams, the second president, and his son, John Quincy, the sixth president; William Henry Harrison, the ninth president and his grandson, Benjamin Harrison, the 23rd president. Franklin Delano Roosevelt, our 32nd president was a cousin of Theodore Roosevelt, the 26th president. So there is some background.

Another consideration that emerged was that such a program would create a formidable storm of opposition and thus an unstoppable impetus to create a new political party strong enough to win a few elections.

20 – Marital Bliss, Corporate Style

Since the Supreme Court has deemed corporations are people entitled to make contributions to political campaigns, many observers feel there is some justification for extending this premise or right to the social arena.

As corporations have been given theoretical flesh, so to speak, why shouldn't they be allowed to marry? Why shouldn't other "people" have the mutual right to wed corporations? Both abilities, meeting logical and fair play standards, make manifest sense. There would be no conflict with same-sex marriages or civil unions, and the Supreme Court having already issued its judgment, wouldn't be likely to be called on again about this subject.

Such marriages couldn't, of course, produce natural children. But adoptions would be available, and obviously corporations have the deep pockets to support large and extended families.

Divorce would also be possible. Causes for dissolution of a marriage, on the part of corporations might be the usual irreconcilable differences. The other "people" shedding their marriage vows could cite diminution of dividends, dislike of a new ad campaign or product, or even a political stance.

In cases of divorce, the thinking is that "people" should get custody of children with corporate spouses to be responsible for children until their maturity.

Knotty issues arise on whether multiple marriages should be permitted. Can the "people" marry more than one corporation? Can a corporation have many spouses? Some limitations would have to apply.

While there are many potential suitors among the "people" mates among corporations would be more limited. Some corporations would surely be more attractive than others. A way would need to be found to ration marital ties to any one corporation. Currently, many argue for either party to have no more than ten marriages. Others claim this shows an undue Islamic or pagan influence.

Sexual identity is another critical issue and possibly an advantage to the entire process. The "people" have no choice of being either male or female whereas corporations can be either sex as called for, bi-sexual, or effectively neutered. This is another huge advantage that corporations hold. Unlike their "people" partners they wouldn't be party to arguments between couples on any number of mundane topics. Nor would they show signs of aging or other distress factors humans are subject to.

In the same vein, such marriages would not inhibit the harmony the "people" have with traditional marriages. On the contrary, existing or future marital relationships would not be challenged by these corporate tie-ins. Nor would either corporate partner be encumbered with the usual responsibilities of marriage such as holiday get-togethers, dealing with relatives, discussing budgets, putting children to bed, going to Parent-Teacher meetings, etc.

In essence, both parties could enjoy all the non-physical benefits of marriage without worrying about petty arguments and the usual tides of love, desire and respect for a spouse.

Naturally, corporations would also be able to give their spouses spending money, which conceivably could be used for political campaigns. However, Congress might be called upon to put a limitation on this outlay, subject of course to any Supreme Court decision. The high court would likely be called upon to adjudicate the constitutionality of the entire program or just this provision. No tie-in of any kind would be permitted by investments with a corporate spouse.

Some claim that this is a revolutionary change in our political/social lifestyle that deserves serious consideration. Others contend that it's a logical extension of the famous French aphorism that the more things change, the more they stay the same.

Most observers believe that the jury will be out for at least a generation to see how such an extended American family life would fare if such a movement were implemented.

Jack Adler

21 - National Hysteria Index

Fears are common in turbulent eras, and we have no shortage of worries about imminent or potential disasters, both domestically and internationally. Accordingly, as the American public, perhaps stimulated by the media, are prone to alarums of one kind or another, there is a plan afoot to create a "National Hysteria Index" that people can refer to in order to locate their level of anxiety. Awareness, of course, would serve as the first step in combating a disturbing sense of personal alarm.

Consider our national record of fears. Currently, on the domestic scene, there's the possibility of some crazed person armed with assault weapons bursting in at transportation terminals, offices and classrooms and wiping out scores of innocent people. Domestic terrorists crop up alarmingly, with the Boston Marathon bloodbath a recent example. Internationally, scares have soared over North Korea's testing of a long-range ballistic missile that could eventually have a nuclear warhead and be able to hit the West Coast of the U.S. The threat of a nuclear-armed Iran also contributes mightily into the psyche of many people.

The sheer proliferation of countries with nuclear weapons as well as the threat of suitcase nuclear weapons by terrorists comes into play. Worries about infection or death by chemical and biological weapons also manifest themselves in this roster of common concerns. Cyber-terrorism, with hackers stealing valuable government and business secrets, has also contributed to tension.

Space-related scares of meteors and solar flares cruising on projectories close to Earth have also caused apprehension.

Today, the threat of Islamic jihadism is still uppermost in many minds. Tomorrow, given the sad state of our economy, it might be palpitations over China supplanting us as the dominant power on the globe. Doomsayers rage over the eventual disappearance of the dollar and economic chaos and anarchy.

There have been all too many other alarms in our history. Among those in contemporary times were Japanese submarines hitting West Coast ports during World War II. This led to one of the reasons Japanese-Americans, in one of the most shameful acts of our history, were interred in American-style concentration camps. In the Cold War with the Soviet Union, many frights surfaced including the threat of Russian nuclear weapons aimed at us from nearby Cuba. Fears of growing Russian military might stroked the so-called "Missile Gap" and Russia's successful Sputnik fanned the fear that we were losing out in the space race. The specter of communism taking over the world dampened optimism over any sort of lasting peace.

Thanks to the false alarms voiced by Senator McCarthy, an irresponsible demagogue, we worried about Communist agents and sympathizers lurking in every government agency. We feared that the loss of Vietnam to the Vietcong would bring about the entire loss of Southeast Asia. Defeating the Sandinistas in Nicaragua was supposed to be crucial to prevent the "Communists" from infiltrating Texas.

And, of course, the terrorist attack on 9/11 unleashed a torrent of fears that we would suffer more such terrible attacks -- and a massive rush to buy duct tape. As a build-up to our preventive war against Iraq, the public was sent into skitters of concern by talk and actual declarations of "fact" by senior administration officials that Iraq possessed weapons of mass destruction; and that Iraq was tied in to al Qaeda. No such weapons were ever found; nor was any meaningful link with al Qaeda detected.

Not all fears are unfounded or unjustified. Plans for terrorist attacks have been detected in advance and effectively blocked. But it is clear that public sentiments can be manipulated by government and media to the point where hysteria can be a disturbing factor.

This characteristic has led to a hysteria index to indicate when to slow down and let logic overcome emotion. The much abused color index devised to show the level of danger from a terrorist attack had a bunch of light shades that many found too close in their appearance. This hysteria index, also using a quartet of colors, would still work in a different fashion. Black would connote that we've gone off the deep end in total unreasoning obeisance to irrational fears and that we've surrendered to our worst instincts. White, at the other end of the index, would just indicate a minor flush of reasonable uneasiness that could be easily dismissed. Just two colors would lie in-between in the belief that too many colors and color gradations confuse the public. Red would mean a heavy outpouring of unnecessary alarm and a last chance not to succumb to dark, thoughtless misgivings. Blue would indicate a worrisome but still manageable degree of unwelcome agitation.

Proponents also point out how this color scheme, minus the dreaded black, provides a measure of patriotism with use of the familiar red, white and blue.

Critics, though, are expected to have a field day with the national hysteria index, calling it an act of hysteria itself.

Bears thought.

22 - Worldwide Volunteer Army

In medieval times Popes called for volunteers to go on a crusade to the Holy Land and rescue Jerusalem from the Muslims who controlled the area. Many nobles, warriors and other men, and the inevitable camp followers, answered their call and marched to the edge of Europe and took sail to the Holy Land to wage battle.

Consider the possibilities of a modern counterpart. What would happen if the call went out from religious leaders of all faiths – Islam included – for men and women to volunteer their services in an army that could be called up to strike against any obvious violations to the conscience of the world. Obviously, the United Nations isn't up to this task. Nor is NATO, or like military alliances, likely to come to the fore as quickly or as often as might be needed.

Such an international army could come from all quarters of the world in staging points in North America, South America, Europe, Asia and Africa. At each staging point they could be supplied with arms and then dispatched by air, land and/or sea to the problem area. The equipment and transportation services would be paid for by donations, and there are enough guilty consciences around the world to foot this bill.

Let's take the Rwanda holocaust as an example. Soldiers from a couple of European countries already in Rwanda did little or nothing to stop the systematic slaughter of Tutsi by Hutus. Nothing was done by the United Nations or any international organization. Nearly a million Tutsis died, and the consequences of the tragedy are still being felt in Central Africa, especially in the

Congo area bordering on Rwanda. Governments and politicians around the world did nothing, and that includes the U.S. President Clinton subsequently apologized for his inaction.

Volunteers within Africa could have congregated at the African staging point, which might be along the Mediterranean coast. If this were the case, the African volunteer continent might be augmented by volunteers from Southern Europe and the Middle East. Once consolidated, such a force could have been transported as promptly as possible to Rwanda. Imagine all the lives that could have been saved, and the avoidance of such a horrible stain on our planet's sad history.

Rules of engagement pose a critical point. Could the volunteers shoot at will or just when fired upon? If they were to be effective, the volunteers would need to be fully authorized to stop violence and defend locals. This means they don't have to wait until they're fired on to take effective action. Their mission, whatever it might be, would be crippled otherwise.

Consider the horrors of the Serbian ethnic cleaning in Bosnia-Herzogovina and Kosovo. Especially recall the tragedy that took place at Srebrinica where Dutch NATO. troops stood aside, under the limitation of the rules of engagement imposed on them while hundreds of Bosnian Muslim males were lined up and systematically killed. Under this program, such a horrific massacre might have been avoided or blunted.

If such holocausts are to be prevented, immediate action needs to be taken and not subject to the frustrating dithering of governments and the difficulties of consensus at the U.N.'s Security Council.

Clearly, such a volunteer force can't go into every country. Neither China nor Russia, each having dissident ethnic groups under their control (Tibetan and Muslims in Sinkiang Province in China, and the Chechens and other ethnic groups in the Caucasus Mountains area of Russia), will vote for this program or allow entry into their respective countries. Similarly, many nations facing internal turmoil will resist what they consider a violation of their territory. But will they actually shoot at a determined and well-armed international voluntary army that is likely to be primarily composed of dedicated men and women from many countries, and possibly even their own nation? The more likely stance will be a call for negotiations that could end the need for a continued intervention. Even the threat of such a force being deployed could suffice to stem conflicts.

Many issues would have to be decided including age limitations, if women could be part of the force, any payments to volunteers, suppliers and others involved in the training and movement of such an assembled fighting force. Setting up who would command the volunteer army and how officers would be selected would also be important factors to handle.

The U.N., of course, would never sanction such a volunteer force. Its sanctions, unfortunately, have less impact. But if the will is there among a decent number of nations, such a volunteer army can work.

Let the call go out and see what the response is.

23 – Punditry

You don't need a license to be a pundit. You just need an audience, which used to be limited mostly to print outlets – newspapers and magazines – or electronically with television and radio. With the growth of the Internet, more opportunities to share your opinions, or less charitably, your pontifications, have merged. The advent of blogs have made us a nation of would-be pundits. In fact, anyone with any measure of an audience can declare him or herself, or have others do the honor, to be a pundit. Professional pundits are often paid, but not always.

Pundit is derived from the Hindi word, "pandit" which means "learned man." There may be a valid reason for the switch in the initial vowel. Many of today's pundits can probably be challenged on just how learned they are, but one doesn't reach the exalted status of being a pundit overnight. Generally, one has to amass a credible amount of credits on a given subject or range of subjects. There is no set standard for when one reaches the magic land of punditry.

One can achieve a reputation of sorts, possibly through publication of newspaper/ magazine columns, or books. Subsequently, the opinions of this contender to pundit status is given all due respect. This sort of responsibility can conjure the need or desire on the part of pundits to maintain or advance their punditry stature with more and more daring outbursts. The road to punditry ascendance is strewn with flawed notions and observations.

Given the influence pundits may yield – and there is no way to calculate their individual impact on the public – it's high time something was done to produce greater order. Accordingly, here are some possibilities.

Television shows strain for the best ratings, which of course can influence how much advertising dollars come their way. Why not apply a comparable system to how pundits fare? Such a rating would help determine their presence on any shows or programs and any invitations to share their viewpoints. The same system that rates television shows can be adapted to rate pundits who appear on the tube.

But a larger system is needed to entail print and other electronic outlets.

Polls seem to be taken on so many subjects. Why not a poll on various pundits? The larger the number of poll participants, the better. As the way questions are designed can determine the results of a poll, it may be necessary to have a select committee of university journalism professors handle this tricky assignment.

It may be too much to require an academic degree for one to be recognized as a pundit, beyond the more self-congratulatory elements of Internet exposure. How well one does in school doesn't always prefigure success in the commercial world. But it would certainly offer a measure of support for the editorial heft of a candidate for punditry. Someone with a degree in punditry would surely have a leg up on other scholastically deprived suitors for prize spots in media. Such an academic course could be offered under the aegis of journalism departments. Imagine Punditry I and II courses added to some curriculums.

Furthermore, imagine sitting before your television set and watching a man or woman deliver stinging opinions on a politician or government policy and having greater faith in the wisdom of this so-called pundit. Or reading a newspaper or magazine and absorbing the calculated wisdom of a truly accredited pundit.

This is a worthwhile goal.

Accreditation can be denoted by a short notice, possibly in parentheses, that the writer has been recognized as a pundit by whatever name is given to the organization handling such recognitions. In time, a symbol or icon might be attached to a name to indicate this writer has reached such an august stage.

As the number of pundits rise so does the need for an intelligent and responsible system of sorting out this opinion-laden group.

24 - Sister Couples

Brotherhood, sisterhood, and like hoods (except perhaps for some urban examples) can all help bond countries, cities, and people together. But we ought to look to see how the concept can help in the treatment of social situations. While some states have moved forward to allow same sex marriages, others adhering to the supposed sanctity of traditional marriage as only between a man and woman have held back, though public opinion has swung in favor of such unions. The United States, supposed to be in the forefront of freedom for individuals, lags well behind other nations when it comes to the same sex marriage issue.

Here's one such plan for consideration involving same sex couples that may persuade disapproving states to reconsider their positions.

Some American cities have sister cities abroad. Among examples are: New York that includes Cairo, Budapest, Jerusalem and Johannesburg among its urban relatives; and Los Angeles which counts Auckland, Berlin, Nagoya and Mexico City among its sisterly brethren.

It's a program that promotes worldwide harmony and solidarity, with both cities sending representatives to each other and conducting various social and art programs in unison. The same principle can be applied to the thorny and contentious issue of same-sex couples.

Here's how it could work.

Every unmarried same-sex couple would be assigned a traditional couple as a sister couple (or brother couple if preferred) in the same city, and as much as possible in the same part of the city. Match-ups can be made, as much as possible, for couples with or without children, with age and occupation taken into consideration.

In this fashion, worries in some conservative quarters that same-sex couples – and worse their marriage or even their civil union – will eventually crush traditional marriage will be reduced. It will be obvious to all concerned that both couples lead similar and normal daily lives. Their children will bond first and then their "parents." Camaraderie will develop, and the country will draw closer -- even if some politicians and demagogues don't -- with one less divisive issue.

Consider how such units will do things together, such as shop, have dinner parties, go to movies and sports events, car pool, and sundry other potential tie-ins. Their children may play together. Even taking vacations together would be a distinct possibility.

All pairings would be made by a municipal administrator, with the city, state and federal government dividing the cost that has to be considered minimal when weighing the potential benefits to be derived. Each pairing would be made for a two-year period that can be renewable, and many such relationships would doubtless lead to permanent friendships. Two years should be plenty of time for couples to fully get to know each other. The pairings would be subject to monitoring on a regular basis by the staff of the municipal administrator. The frequency of such checks would up to local administrations.

However, parties would not be held to a contract. Either couple could leave the relationship at any time, though they would be counseled to stick it out.

This sister family program will unite America as never before, and once again be a shining beacon of tolerance to the rest of the world. The "Declaration of Independence" would take on greater and more contemporary resonance and meaning. Note the point of "again" as some figures in our national life in recent years have hardly served as a role model for other peoples and nations.

This is an idea whose value and readiness is palpable. "Sister couples" can be a valuable conduit to greater social harmony.

God, and the country alike, know we need it.

25 - Dictators & Education

While some political figures, as well as educators, might rail at the notion of courses that don't hail the United States as ever virtuous in its dealings with other nations, there is ample evidence in our history that provide a more realistic appraisal of American activities. Such factual material, while likely to be controversial in some quarters, can actually improve rather than diminish our sense of patriotism. Here's one course that merits attention.

"Dictators" is a new course that should be considered for high school students.

The course, sure to be contentious, can be designed to present a more sobering portrayal of American history. The U.S. has opposed some foreign dictators and backed others. This course will explain the inconsistency.

Tyrants who satisfied our interests received military aid, loans, and other support while we overlooked their transgressions, such as basic human rights, over their own people. No matter how repressive the regime, our administrations closed their collective eyes as long as a dictator was against Communists and allowed American companies to make money in their countries. American corporations gobbled up huge tracts of foreign land, paid peon wages, and subsidized cooperative "leaders."

Only when their regimes became too difficult to prop up, give an uprising or two, did the U.S. back away.

As the saying went about these tarnished leaders abroad, "He may be a son-of-a-bitch, but he's our son-of-a-bitch."

This is the truth, and no amount of denial will remove the reality. Yet this aspect of our history is seldom taught, certainly not at the high school level.

To review some examples, the U.S. condoned the corrupt regime of Ferdinand Marcos in The Philippines, mainly to secure our military bases there such as at Subic Bay. Eventually, the Filipinos had enough of the dictator and he was driven into exile. Our naval base at Subic Bay is gone, too.

Similarly, for many years we tolerated Fulgencio Batista as the corrupt ruler of Cuba, conveniently overlooking his tie-ins with organized crime. Finally, a revolution led to Batista fleeing the country. His successor, Fidel Castro vaulted into power. But as his political sympathies were clearly left-wing and inclined toward a form of Communism, we opposed him with sanctions that have lasted for decades despite their ineffectiveness; and we even planned his assassination which was bungled. Worse, a land invasion of Cuba was an embarrassing failure.

In the Middle East the U.S. has supported regimes, like the Saudi Arabian princes, who permit little of the democracy we piously espouse in order to secure their oil and their support against first Communism and now terrorism. Ironically, more terrorists involved in 9/11 came from Saudi Arabia than any other country. Originally, the U.S. gave its support to Saddam Hussein, despite his brutal treatment of his own people including the gassing of Kurdish villages; only when Saddam overplayed his hand by invading Kuwait did we seek his overthrow.

The course would also cover situations where we've helped depose legal governments. In Iran we helped overthrow the nationalist, Mohammad Mossadegh, who wanted to nationalize the foreign-owned oil companies. In his place we helped install Shah Pahlavi who ran the country like a dictator until he was forced to flee. We're still suffering from the results of this coup we plotted and carried out.

In Guatemala we orchestrated the downfall of Jacobo Arbenz, the legal president of the Central American country. He only wanted to secure the assets of Guatemala for the Guatemalans, which didn't sit well with American economic interests. Salvador Allende was the lawful president of Chile, but his socialist policies were anathema to Washington. The U.S. assisted in a coup that led to Agosto Pinochet becoming the right-wing dictator of Chile until he was forced to leave - but only after many of his Chilean opponents had been killed by his repressive regime.

And so on. This class isn't meant to denigrate the U.S. but only to give students an honest and more balanced rendition of U.S. history, and one that will enable them to better understand some of the hatred and distaste felt for the U.S. in other parts of the world.

The U.S. is presented, for the most part, in our educational scheme as a force for good in the world. This course would produce more citizens to make this belief a truth based on reality and not a false reading of history.

What are the chances of such a course making its way into our high school curriculums?

Don't bet on it.

26 - Reforming The Draft

Hopefully, the United States will never need to reintroduce a draft into our army.

But if one is implemented again it should be done on a fairer basis which certainly includes less deferments for the well-connected. Meanwhile, some redress should be instituted to make up for past transgressions. While we may not need a national draft to reach certain manpower figures for each branch of our armed forces, we do need a draft to lessen the ongoing stigma of a national disgrace.

When there was a draft, too many of our better connected men and youths escaped any duty, or avoided combat duty with softer home-based assignments. One need look no further than former President George W. Bush who landed a cushy National Guard posting; evidently, he never actually completed his term of duty, managing to slip away from service for a considerable amount of time. And then there's former Vice President Dick Cheney, he of "Make the world safe for Halliburton fame", who openly admitted that he sought and received numerous deferments during the Vietnam War as he had other "priorities" than serving his country as many of his countrymen did. Not to be accused of any partisan fervor, former President Bill Clinton also falls into this category of those not too disposed to embrace military service.

It's no secret that our armed services are disproportionately filled with African-American and Hispanic youths and those from the more economically disadvantaged part of our population. There have been murmurings of dissent and cries for redress, even by a Congressman; but nothing has been done.

Affirmative action is supposed to compensate African-Americans for the deprivations suffered in the past by giving them a leg up today in the academic and business worlds. What is needed now is a two-part affirmative action to remedy the draft ills foisted on the nation by the high and the mighty.

Here are some ideas to consider.

One, offspring of draft age of everyone in the federal branch, especially the children of senators, congressmen, cabinet heads, judges and like figures should immediately be put into service for a two year period if not already serving in this fashion (and there are notable examples of those who have served and are serving with distinction). This group can also encompass high-level officials, elected and otherwise, in state, county and municipal offices around the country.

Keep in mind that members of the British royal family serve in their armed forces and have even faced combat. We should do no less. These draftees can serve at will in the military rather than in one unit. This policy would promote more camaraderie among elements of our population, and certainly generate much less grumbling about essential fairness. Cohesiveness in combat situations would follow as a natural consequence.

Second, every major official who escaped the draft in the past should be allowed to make up for their evasion of military service by serving now in some capacity. The time frame of such service, to avoid any undue harshness, could be trimmed somewhat. If out of office, the service can start immediately; if still in office, as soon as they leave their duties. Age and health would be taken into consideration but not stop suitable service from being found. The most notable members of such a group are clearly President Bush and Vice President

Cheney. Bush can make up for his National Guard service, not by flying jets but by maintenance work on one of our aircraft carriers; he might even mount a sign, "Mission Being Finally Accomplished." Cheney, in deference to his weak heart, can serve in a mess hall on one of our staging centers in Kuwait or at Bagram Air Force Base in Afghanistan while it's still open. If closed, we have many other military installations around the world that would be honored by having someone like him helping out in the mess hall. Instead of tossing out certitudes that many question he can toss out food no one questions to our service men and women.

Like the famed legal aphorism, fairness delayed is fairness denied.

27 - Youth & Politics

Politicians do a good job of taking care of themselves with salary increases not always subject to public scrutiny in advance and not always well publicized afterwards; health coverage far better than most Americans have; trouble-free and generous pensions; and assorted other benefits. Still, attracting the best and the brightest to enter the field is not always easy. Here is one solution to remedy this situation.

The prospect of young people no longer being attracted to the field of politics is due to a large extent as a byproduct of various scandals including Watergate and Iran-Contra. The public at large has a large and festering doubt about the veracity and dedication to the public welfare of its representatives in office. That they elected these questionable leaders is the cruelest irony.

Given the current image people have of politics, there's no way to depend on truly conscientious and idealistic young people voluntarily seeking a career in politics, or even working in it for short periods. Like water seeking the lowest level politics attracts too many whose ethics can't survive the temptations thrown at them. But this country can't keep affording this type of loss, so there is some sentiment for implementing a political youth conscription program.

It's a draft for political, not military, service. We can't depend on volunteers, either in numbers or with the stamina of their political purity.

Here's how the draft would work.

It would be set up on an equitable basis between top students, those with the highest grades in any subjects, not just liberal arts subjects. Leanings toward any political party will not be a factor in selection. Without sacrificing quality it's essential to make sure that the PDs or political draftees are drawn from every part of the country and every class of people. Good connections wouldn't be a factor.

One option in the selection process is to allocate a quota of 100 college graduates with the best overall record, academically and otherwise, from each state per academic semester. Then these graduates would be subject to interviews with a certain number, still to be established, drafted. They would be drafted for two years, exactly the same as if they were drafted into the army. Politically speaking, as it were, we're in a war-time situation with the terrorism threat. So there is a need to train our young for political leadership as well as how to handle AK-47s.

The political draftees would be given paid internship positions that would show them how governments are run and thus to prepare them for higher positions in government later. Their status, however, would be substantially higher than the current role given to government interns who generally seek these positions. Of course, there is the very real fear that the PDs might be so turned off by what they see going on that they will disdain any thought of a career in politics. This counter argument also poses the cogent question: if these graduates were drafted into political service, how would this inspire them to want to stay in politics? How many military draftees reenlist in the army?

Accordingly, there will also be special inducements for political reenlistment. Raises will certainly be possible as well as promotions based on merit. At the end of their term of duty, they'll get medals – possibly a Lavender Heart - for their service with the underlying understanding that they showed heroism in resisting temptations that surely came their way. One way or another, we'll reward those who withstand the system.

Many observers deny the argument that such medals, if worn, would bring excessive attention to this new brand of political veterans. No one is so callous that we don't realize how induction into politics could prejudice a young person's reputation and career. After all, we want the PDs to be able to achieve as normal a life as possible if they choose not to continue in politics after their period of service.

These are realistic concerns. Cries for sacrifice and dedication to country will fall flat. There are times when a country in war, and we're in an asymmetric war with the forces of terrorism, has to impose a system. This is such a time. This country can't afford to lose entire generations of wise and honest leadership because current crops of bright college graduates look down with justifiable cause on the political arena. They, like all of us, have to sacrifice themselves for the good of the nation.

Bear a burden, bear the system!

28 - Renditions In Reverse

The United States has taken a considerable amount of criticism for its involvement in the practice of "rendition" and our concept of torture. Our denials to the contrary, there is ample proof of our complicity in sending "suspects" to Middle Eastern nation, sometimes with the aid of some European governments who either provided specific help or conveniently looked the other way.

Here is a way to make up for some of the excesses we're held responsible for around the world, and to some extent, in our country as well. The commitment to basic fairness would be a tremendous boost to our national image.

Under the policy of rendition, persons the U.S. took into "custody" abroad were then quickly and mysteriously transported to another country where their treatment, shall we say, was far less humane – but still considered to be more effective in obtaining information and intelligence than our softer methods. Torture of these so-called suspects, which has been amply documented, was often more than just a distinct possibility. Of course, the U.S. doesn't torture people. We just redefine the meaning of torture to suit our purposes.

Other than the sheer inhumanity of the process, mistaken identifications have been made with the wrong person hooded, prodded, shackled, drugged, and mishandled by Americans while being flown elsewhere and then dumped into some dank prison to await far from painless interrogations. The premise of their imprisonment, of course, is that they wouldn't be there if they weren't guilty and didn't have valuable information to reveal. It isn't guilt until innocence is proven; it's just guilt.

Our image, naturally, has taken a considerable beating around a good part of the world. America the beautiful had let the threat of terrorism turn it into America the torture accomplice. Some Americans were convicted in absentia in Italy for their part in the taking of a suspect. Legal redress in our court –with the usual refrain of state secrets being at risk of disclosure - was denied to another man who was finally released when it was realized he wasn't the right person at all. Of course, by this time he was a shell of his former self.

Now the time has come for some version of international fair play, rendition in reverse. But not in a fashion that mimics the gross kidnappings that have taken place on alleged suspects. Under "rendition in absentia," Americans, too, can experience the horror and degradation though not the sheer physical pain and the indignity of being shoved into a vehicle off the street or any location and driven to an airport for transport to a number of countries with outstanding records for humane interrogation methods,

This is how this new system, sure to be applauded by many and damned by others, would work. Suppose a foreign nation suspected an American of what they considered to be terrorist activities, but they had no proof, no indictment, or anything of that nature. Standard extradition, certainly on such a slim basis, wouldn't work. Sterner measures would be considered to be the only way to get the desired evidence. But interrogation by solely by American methods and Americans would be out of favor.

The foreign government would then submit a request for rendition to our state department. If approved, the person in question would then be subject to being videotaped as he, or she, was kidnapped off the streets and carted off to a place of interrogation – but at a secret U.S. location. To give a foreign imprimatur to the operation, a Canadian or Mexican location might be used if either of those countries approved.

At this happy place, the American would be drilled but not by an American interrogator. A national of the foreign nation would do the honors, even though not on his native soil. However, only the American-approved methods of torture (also known as "enhanced interrogation techniques") could be applied. These efforts might include constant loud music, lights turned on all the time, simulated water-boarding, humiliation by opposite sex interrogators, etc.

The whole procedure, limited perhaps to no more than two or three days of pseudo imprisonment, would be videotaped with copies to the foreign government and our own government. Doctors would be on hand, naturally, to insure that interrogation not be excessively detrimental to the detainee's health. The results, positive or negative in gaining the sought after information, would remain a secret. So would the identity of the American and the foreign government.

After all, mistakes are made.

29 - Culture Wars Champions

Much is written about the severity of the culture wars besetting the country. We have, in the estimation of some observers, two nations divided by more than the same language. In fact, it isn't even certain the same meanings are attached to words by the warring factions. It's not like the issue of slavery hardening the differing resolves of the North and South prior to and during the Civil War. Nor is it the lingering discord after the war and then the advent of the broad issue of civil rights.

But the current situation is poisonous on a different level, perhaps because it doesn't have, presumably, a military or real war outlet. Somehow not ridding your opponents lethally serves to make all other avenues of interactions more venomous.

It's not as if elements of stark cultural differences haven't been with us on a continual basis, but the concept of cultural wars is relatively new. Its sting was enhanced by a presidential aspirant several elections ago making a big deal out of different viewpoints on such subjects as abortion, gun control, same sex marriage, immigration, et al. Different perspectives of these and like subjects certain existed, and still do, but it has taken the last couple of decades for positions to stiffen into groups waging a "war."

The enmity – which, collectively, is "us" - not only exists but festers. Contrasting viewpoints aren't going to go away. But that doesn't mean we can't organize a palliative arrangement to defuse the rancor.

One suggestion shows a historical structure. In ancient times, and up to medieval days, opposing armies might choose a champion from their ranks. This warrior would then meet his counterpart from the other army in single combat. The winner of this fight would signal which army was the victor. This sort of battle saved many lives from both armies.

Some examples: David versus Goliath in the biblical story; Roland against Olivier in the medieval French epic; and Sohrab fighting his father, Rustem, in the Persian tale. But there are others in the annals of warfare.

Accordingly, the thought is to enlist a champion from both sides. They can meet in a telegenic field of combat, not just once but often. They could trade arguments and barbs instead of dodging lances and swords. Being a "champion" would be a role available on an equal gender basis. Essentially, these would be debates, but the difference would come through two factors: changing personalities and the frequency of the debates. Instead of the same champion representing each side at each meeting, there could be some variation.

However, the same "champion" could appear more than once, just not all the time. The frequency under consideration is monthly. It's felt that a monthly battle would keep the issues alive in a healthy fashion rather than their lying hidden, to some extent, in people's minds.

The famed pre-Civil War debates between Abraham Lincoln and Stephen Douglas (who both had presidential aspirations), which were more speeches on the same or similar subjects, might be another example. But in this scenario, multiple candidates would face off against each in the glare of television and before audiences at home throughout the country.

Unlike a presidential debate, there isn't any need for someone to serve as the person asking questions of each speaker. One issue could be the entire topic of each meeting that should run an hour and during prime time.

It's hoped that the networks would offer free time; but if not, the federal government, could fund the debates. It's conceivable that some companies – not just one – but a group to show some semblance of joint responsibility might also be sponsors. But other than a simple acknowledgment of their generosity, there would be no other commercials of any sort.

Each speaker could respond to the other, challenging each his or her opponent's point of view rather than talking to viewers. Their actual speaking times could be limited to no more than ten minutes per response. Each speaker would be guaranteed half of the hour time.

Jarring mental torpor from the populace, and providing useful nuances to the issue, should prove to be highly beneficial. At least, each side would receive – in a peaceful setting - a good idea of their opponent's point of view.

The cultural war may not end with such programming. It may even become more entrenched. But the country itself will be better off, with the champions lashing out at each other only to change minds.

And, of course, one can always change channels.

30 - Designated Or Dual President Rule

Perhaps there's another way to improve our political fortunes. Democracy, as has been stated by Winston Churchill, is supposed to be the worst form of government except for all the others. But then we don't have a democracy; we have a republic; and we have the Electoral College instead of a direct vote. Nor do we have a parliamentary system where an administration can be voted out of office before its official term of office is over no matter how disastrous its policies have been. Issues like these prompt remedial options.

Here is one possible remedy.– the DPR or Designated Pinch-President Rule – to improve the efficiency of the presidency.

As shown by the American baseball league, the public likes the designated hitter rule. It brings more action to the game and, more importantly, it brings a more efficient hitter at the plate to bang out home runs and other base hits and win games With the DPR we can win more important games.

While some might deride putting baseball on the same level as the presidency, the same principle is involved. We have to get the best man up, at the presidency or at the plate. The president, of course, is the most powerful person on the planet. At truly critical moments it may be prudent to have an optimum person yielding— in some cases—sharing this power. The likelihood is that sharing will be considered the wiser policy.

Let's look at this possible program realistically. Say we're in a real economic hassle, like inflation and recession at the same time, or Wall Street has invented a new kind of derivative to put the worldwide economy in another downspin. With the DPR in effect, we can elevate an economic expert as the temporary co-president with equal standing to voice opinions, suggest executive decisions, use the bully pulpit, etc.

Many might ask why can't the real president just get the opinion of this expert and use it himself.

The answer, as it is so often is, comes down to politics. Will the sitting president really try to get this expert, who might be in a different political party, to be of aid? Might this expert of a different political hue not want to help a president he or she wants to fail? And, lastly, will the president use the expert's opinion if it differs from his own? Presidents usually get good advice from their cabinets and advisers, but do they always follow it.

With the DPR, there's no doubt that the best brains of the country will be used for each particular problem. Keep in mind, though, that the president would stay in his elected office. In baseball when a player is hit for he's out of the game unlike in football and basketball where players can be freely substituted. Professional sports has some lessons to teach our political mentors. The president can always contribute his opinion, so in effect, we have two presidents, an expert and a generalist. The program can be invoked by a two-thirds vote of both houses of Congress for every conceivable problem, once an issue reaches a significant level affecting the prosperity and security of the nation.

Congress would have to approve this seminal change in our political structure, and it will take a major bipartisan effort. A majority vote in both the House of Representatives and the Senate should be sufficient. No filibuster would be permitted. A key factor will be the length of time given the DPR. The program, except for more stringent time allowances, is akin to having a special investigator appointed to get to the bottom of national scandals. Any proposal by the DP would have to be approved as well by Congress.

A strong campaign will be needed to educate the public and to avoid undue worries about a coup or confusion at the White House. The more politically attuned might argue that such an arrangement would upset the constitutional balance of power between the executive branch and the Congress.

But safeguards can be inserted into the program. The president could veto any of the DPs, which could be overridden by two-thirds of the Senate just like now. The sitting president might take a back seat to the DP but he would still stay in his elected office. Far from creating a new system of government the DPR builds upon our existing constitutional structure and utilizes the national pastime at the same time.

What could be more promising and patriotic at the same time?

31 – American Sharia

The so-called "clash of civilizations" is a frightful specter looming over the world. But there may be ways to lessen the differences between Islam and the West.

As words are borrowed from one language to another, and certainly English has many words from other tongues including Arabic, social/religious practices can also be implemented in a blended fashion.

Sharia, the Islamic code used by Muslim fundamentalists, provides harsh penalties for those found guilty of various misdeeds from simple theft to adultery.

The severe punishments – beheadings, stoning to death, amputations of arms and other appendages -- shock western sensibilities. Inception of Sharia in nations threatened with, or already under fundamental Islamic control, constitutes a major concern for the U.S. and its allies.

To a lesser extent, some critics contend that terrorists and their cries of "jihad" have hijacked a religion. Surely not every Muslim is a fundamentalist and/or a jihadist, but it is equally clear that elements of the religion do permit an aggressive approach to making converts – and a heavenly reward in Nirvana for their efforts. Moreover, Islam is spreading, and in some countries in Europe, the Muslims have been decidedly slow in assimilation.

There is a way to alleviate all these worries and problems, and perhaps blend the west and Islam (where religion often is the state, unlike the west) in a felicitous fashion that can satisfy more fundamentalists and probably most moderate Muslims faithful to their religion.

We should institute an American version of Sharia, which can then be adapted to other countries like France, Germany, Netherlands, etc. Such a movement requires much thought and great care in implementation. Of course, we can't and shouldn't employ severe punishments, which would be unconstitutional anyhow. But we can mold a tough code on an ecumenical basis that shows respect for all religions.

American Sharia might recall, for some, bygone eras of Puritanism and Scarlet Letter days. But the symbolism involved might well lessen the woes of dramatically apposite cultures.

Here are some thoughts. First, no additional punishments would be meted out beyond normal civil and criminal punishments. American Sharia will not be a substitute for our normal system of law. However, certain offences can mean consequences. Suppose one seriously and evilly blasphemes (with what constitutes blasphemy given a liberal interpretation), and against any religion, including Islam? Such a person could be put into a public pillory on television for a set period of time. Reverend Pat Robertson, not too long ago, uttered some blasphemous comments about Islam. Consider what the image of Robertson in a pillory, shown on television and in photos, around the world would do to improve the overall image of the U.S., so much in free fall these days. The same would be true for a certain Florida pastor who set out to burn the Koran, the holy book of Islam.

Humiliation, which can include a public spanking as opposed to flogging, can serve as a soft or subdued physical form of punishment for many moral offences. Affixing a scarlet letter to one's clothing for a certain amount of time is still an effective measure of punishment. So is tarring and feathering and shunning, though the former does seem to be cruel and inhuman punishment and thus unconstitutional. A modern form of shunning may be worked out.

None of these punishments would be forever. Nor would American Sharia include any form of "fatwa" such as Islamic ayatollahs and imams charging their faithful with killing writers and cartoonists they deem to have mocked their religion in some way. But American Sharia would have enormous symbolic value in showing our mutual beliefs and values. After all, we share a belief in a monotheistic God. American Sharia might well be a tool to mend a growing divide. At the very least the word "Sharia" might not invoke visions of a dread system of justice.

Commensurate consideration from the Islamic world would be expected, with western values allowed to meld with Koranic edicts.

Saving souls, as well as a few limbs, can be a joint effort.

32 - Immigration Reversed

Immigration from south of the border is obviously a major and thorny issue. The United States has to come up with a sensible and practical way of handling the festering situation which includes so many illegal people living in the U.S. Heartbreaking cases of families being separated, parents deported while their American-born children are left behind, occur all too frequently. The problems and complications are stupendous, while Republicans and Democrats spar over their respective positions.

Finally, coping with a major legislative challenge, Congress has changed our immigration policy and for the better; but not enough to suit everyone, and there's still more that can be done.

Here's one possible way to ameliorate the situation.

Immigration can, of course, be a two-way street. Amazingly, no one has come up with a solution which is sure to defuse this divisive issue which has roiled the republic.

No matter how much of a manned fortress we construct on our border with Mexico, people seeking better lives are still going to try to get through and many will probably succeed. But this program will reduce fatalities suffered by those from south of the border who don't make it through the harsh deserts, rat-infested tunnels, and betrayals by "coyotes" – those individuals who extract exorbitant fees from people seeking entry to the U.S. Less deaths would also occur with our valiant border guards whose difficult job is not always fully appreciated.

Those "illegals" already here, and who have made a life for themselves in the U.S., are understandably loath to leave. Whatever solution, if any, emerges on this group – said to be eleven million strong – there is still another way to redress the balance of people on both sides of the border. Helping to adjust the nation's balance of payments might well be another benefit of this proposal.

We need a force of volunteers to emigrate to Mexico, obtain dual citizenship, and work there for a set amount of time. This process would raise the general standard of living in Mexico which, in turn, would mean less Mexicans will want to come to the U.S. Our transplanted Americans will surely achieve a level of well-being in Mexico. In fact, some may become more prosperous in Mexico than they ever were or likely to become in the U.S.

This group can be drawn from the disadvantaged in the U.S., the unemployed, the less skilled, etc. The impact would clearly lead to a meaningful lessening of our unemployed rolls. Mexico would experience an influx of labor and not just an infusion of our less valued or skilled people. Many of the unemployed are quite skilled in various fields, but may have been laid off due to technological changes and changing economic and market conditions.

However, the project is not intended to add unemployment in Mexico, which would defeat the purpose. Possibly a joint Mexican-American unemployment stipend can be given to the emigrants to tide them over until they find work or create jobs through their own entrepreneurial efforts.

Nor would the program entail shipping any criminals or mentally defective people to Mexico. Everyone dispatched would be a reasonable candidate for temporary relocation.

Another key aspect of the project calls for a certain number of American employers – drawn to a certain extent from those who had employed Mexicans in the U.S. on an illegal basis – to set up businesses/outlets in Mexico and to employ this new work force at American wage levels. However, half of the new jobs would have to go to Mexicans.

The volunteers would sign a contract for five years. Their relocation costs would be borne equally by the American and Mexican governments. Similarly, the employers would sign a contract to keep their Mexican outlets open for at least five years, but they would handle their own relocation costs as the price for their previous malfeasance.

Culturally, this move would bind the two most populous nations in North America closer together. English would certainly become more widely spoken in Mexico, and there would likely be less clamor in the U.S. for English to be declared the official tongue of the country as the Spanish-speaking Hispanic element in our population grows. Eventually, many more people in both countries would become bilingual.

'Que viva imigracion' – but in both directions.

Jack Adler

33 – "Reconciliation U.S.A"

National reconciliation took center stage in South Africa after the end of the Apartheid era. Much has been written about this program, and its successes in helping the people in South Africa of different colors to bond together. Several movies have also been produced. However, a similar plan with less dramatic overtones has been drawn for the U.S.

Tailored somewhat after the successful reconciliation program in South Africa where lethal-minded proponents of apartheid were given official forgiveness upon open admission of their misdeeds, the American version has been designed to have a similar impact on cleansing the past which might encompass a number of serious issues.

Under this plan, notables of various stripes would come forward before a national reconciliation court to confess their transgressions. Proceedings would be televised to allow the public to share in this process of elevating the national character.

The possible agenda could easily include a succession of ex-presidents and other high officials. If such a program had been in existence, consider this potential roster (only if the luminaries had agreed to participate). Gerald Ford might finally have admitted – if such were the case - that he had secretly pledged to pardon President Nixon if he accepted the need to resign. Nixon himself would have had a great deal to apologize for and several sessions might have been needed. Then Bush senior could have confessed—if a confession was called for - that he was very much in the loop about the hostages/Iran-Contra imbroglio, despite his fervent denials. Reagan would have had to finally come to clean that he did know – if indeed he did - what was going on with the plan to get arms to the Nicaraguan rebels; and perhaps he could apologize for equating the Sandinistas or rebels with our "Founding Fathers."

In addition, Reagan would have needed to disclose – if this is what had happened - that there was some secret understanding about delaying the release of the American captives in Teheran until he was safely elected president in 1980. Moreover, the elder Bush would freely admit pardoning his Secretary of Defense Cabinet member, Casper Weinberger, if he was as complicit as he was in the illegal scheme of arms for hostages. But, again, only if this scenario was a true rendering of the facts in this matter.

President Carter could have argued that he had nothing to own up to but might have finally conceded – if this matched the reality of the moment - that he had been willing to soften his stand on nuclear limitations as well as being a champion of human rights to get the Soviet Union out of Afghanistan. In turn, President Clinton would apologize for deliberately lying about his involvement with several women including Paula Jones and Monica Lewinsky. He might also profess regrets to English language purists on his linguistic contortions in explaining away his guilt.

Lesser figures would also get their liberating time in the dock. Vice President Cheney might show some regret in his assertions of "priority" in not serving in the military. Admiral Poindexter and Oliver North would confess their role in planning and conducting the arms for hostages/Iran-Contra mess. Kevin Starr would outline how he orchestrated a legal trap for Clinton and purposefully embarrassed him in his salacious report, while Paula Jones might confess that she did, indeed, not exactly reject President Clinton's attentions. These assertions would all depend on luminaries vouching for the accuracy of their actions being unveiled in the reconciliation program.

The list goes on and on. Would Condoleezza Rice actually admit to needlessly worrying the American public about mushroom clouds out of Iraq when Saddam Hussein didn't have any WMD, a fact well reported to the administration prior to her declaration? Would George Tenet admit, as some charge, that as head of the CIA he failed to give President Bush the full truth about intelligence concerning Iraq? Or, as some assert, he gave Bush the "truth" Bush wanted to hear.

On the non-political front, the procession of famous athletes owning up to drug use would be restorative to the purity of the national spirit as well.

A solid amount of good feeling might ensue, doing wonders perhaps to diminish the bitter partisan gridlock in Washington D.C. This reconciliation program could really unite the United States. Members of all religions and political persuasions would come together as never before.

No approval is needed by Congress. Little funding would be required to establish a forum for the reconciliation sessions. Maximum media coverage would be likely.

"Reconciliation U.S.A.", given our current crop of potential candidates, would surely have a bright future.

34 - GRIN or Gambling On Inflation

People gamble over everything. Money is usually involved but not always. Lotteries, with huge payouts, are popular. Online gambling has a plentiful number of players. Las Vegas, Atlantic City and other cities and sites that offer gambling outlets draw a constant flow of visitors. Off-shore vessels offer gaming tables while sea-going cruise ships have ample lounges to try Lady Luck. Enter many supermarkets and some gambling options can be utilized.

Obviously, there is no shortage of opportunities to see how one can overcome the odds against their coming out ahead.

Our justified concern over the threat of inflation, as well as a number of other harmful economic reversals, usually has everyone in a moderate dither. Many approaches have been discussed, and now even one involving gambling has emerged.

The name of the program is GRIN for Gambling 'round Inflation, but it could easily be expanded to cover gas prices, groceries, and even the monthly unemployment rate as well. The premise centers on making more practical use of a national addiction to gambling. In effect, the addiction, such as it is for many, would be used to actually help the economy.

The program would work on a neighborhood basis. Everyone who buys gas at a particular gas station or groceries at a supermarket, could participate. People can, for example, pick a product each week and put in, let's say, $1 in the pot for that week. Then the winners of the kitty that week will be those who picked the product that went up most in price or went down the most. The same scale would apply for gas prices.

The relatively small scale of gambling would be strictly a game of chance with better odds than a lottery. Unlike the ups and down in the stock market, no one would be greatly hurt if they didn't win. Nor would anyone be appreciably enriched if they were winners. But winning even a small amount can generate a better reaction to the dicey aspects of inflation and/or recession. Moreover, the betting wouldn't affect the natural swing of prices, fuel, or employment. Everyone has to shop, many people drive, and most people want jobs.

The program could run on different time frames for products and gas versus such issues as the unemployment rate. The hope is that this program would allow some gambling fun with inflation and related concerns. Naturally, a high-powered public relations campaign would be needed to explain the whole concept. Some concern would surely be voiced that the program just further cements one's willingness to gamble, and is thus immorally catering to individual weakness and contributing to a national blemish.

The plan also entails that one unemployed person per neighborhood or voting district be retained to supervise the program. That's one of the beauties of GRIN as it creates jobs, too. If there isn't a suitable unemployed person the job could go to someone on welfare, so they can get off welfare. The next choice will be someone with the least income, or someone retired on Social Security.

Honorariums to these local administrators would come from the kitty. The program would be entirely self-liquidating. Some people might argue that, under this program, participants would wind up paying for the privilege of losing more money while gambling on inflation. But being able to "grin" through these economic upheavals will be worth the risk for many and take the edge off adverse conditions.

Let's put addictions to gambling to better use.

35 - Pax Americana

Whither Pax Americana?
Has American Exceptionalism exhausted itself?
Are the two notions still related?

It seems clear that the U.S., while still the dominant power in the world (China isn't far behind), is hardly presiding over any sort of peace in this 21st century. Prospects for an American-insured world peace in the future appear gloomy to say the least.

Were such an enforced tranquility to come back, America and whatever allies it could bring with it, would have to militarily coerce other nations. Our experiences in Viet Nam and Afghanistan hardly suggest that the U.S. can call the tune even in small countries. Such dominance ostensibly to insure peace wouldn't fly with China and other large and emerging nations like India and Brazil.

So let's say goodbye to this chimera of a Pax Americana, invented by some neo-conservatives, not all of whom ever served in the military and experienced combat.

Now the U.S. was conceived as an exceptional country. Not everyone in the courts of monarchical Europe expected the American republic to survive. Many did expect, and even hoped for the nation to fall apart as the result of the Civil War. What was clear to any objective scrutiny was that the U.S. behaved pretty much like other nations in pursuit of what it considered its national interests.

Slavery? Why not? Labor was needed for southern plantations. The southwest? Mexico had few people living there and less soldiers to defend the vast territory. It was ours for the taking and we took it. Manifest Destiny was certainly exceptional, only it was less than benign. If we didn't like what was going on in some Latin American nations, especially when there was interference with our economic interests, we sent troops in. If we didn't like duly elected political leaders in a country, we engineered coups. Not so exceptional.

Critics of the United States wonder and carp. National self-regard has its drawbacks.

But the U.S., if it shows a thorough sense of national grit and resolve, can recover some of its luster. We're still deservedly a shining light for much of the world.

However, it should also be recognized that world bodies don't work all that well. The League of Nations, formed after World War I, was obviously ineffective in preventing World War II. Now the United Nations, created after World War II, is much criticized for its inability to prevent and stop genocides, civil wars, and other conflicts. With each world body lack of enforcement authority is credited with being the major cause for institutional weakness. Creation of alliance systems is beginning to resemble pre-Sarajevo in 1914 when England, France, Italy and Russia faced Germany, Austria-Hungary, and Turkey.

The alliance system will only create tension and stalemate, not a true peace. The threat of mutual nuclear destruction is potent but no guarantee of harmony.

The only sort of workable world body would be one with teeth it was willing to use forcefully. In short, peace on such a universal basis would only come through world hegemony. So, in a sense, the much-criticized neo-conservatives were right; only they didn't go far enough. What we need, what the world, needs, is a "World Americana."

Under this new world order, the United States would be dominant as never before. In fact, to carry the neo-conservative theory of American superiority to its logical conclusion, the time has come to supplant the United Nations with the United States of the World. The United Nations would continue to exist, but just for cultural matters, and with even less teeth than it now has.

But the United States could be *primus intra pares*, first among equals. However, with the growing power of China, a dual hegemony is more likely to emerge - a Pax Sino-America.

In this new system, there would be a world president, with rotating American and Chinese presidents. Such a world government, and its president, would have authority to use the armed forces of each nation anywhere. National boundaries, and with it the specter of nationalism to some extent, would vanish. Instead of the dithering of the United Nations, procedural hindrances, vetoes in the Security Council, and ineffectual rules of engagement, this world government could quickly resolve situations like Bosnia, Rwanda, Somalia, and Darfur in Sudan.

The idea of spreading democracy would be abandoned as a relic of discarded political thought. As the ancient Greeks maintained, might makes right. What's truly exceptional is that it takes some more democratic nations – the U.S. primarily - so long to realize and institutionalize this elemental truth.

This epochal change could last for centuries, and even be applied to Outer Space with a United States of the Solar System – again led by an American and Chinese.

Now that would be exceptional.

36 - Senior Commandos

The age at which one is considered a "senior" seems to range between 40 and 70, though that cutoff could tilt in either direction, depending on social attitudes, publishers' thrust for readers and market share, and governmental actions. What to do about the impending financial problems with Social Security payments and Medicare is also plaguing the country. What's clear is that the aged part of society is growing faster than any other segment. We have what is called the "old olds", those living into their eighties and beyond.

The financial aspects can be left to sharper minds (hopefully there are some in Congress). But here's a possible measure to put this growing contingent, with a vast array of skills, to use. Create a Senior Corps that can undertake special assignments, both domestically and internationally. As far as service abroad, these elders can put their mature skills and knowledge to complement the important work accomplished by much more youthful Peace Corp members.

Some seniors – based on their backgrounds and aptitudes - could receive special training as Senior Commandos, ready for quick assignments to help communities struggling with problems. These problems could cover a broad spectrum of situations involving accounting, bookkeeping, educational curriculums, construction and architectural designs, inventory control, etc.

Many valuable deeds could be done, all consonant with the mental and physical capabilities of the newly coined commandos. Not all missions would, of course, be major projects; but many cities, towns and communities around the country who lack the budgets for needed improvements could find such senior commandos an excellent resource.

Senior commandos, to denote their status, could also be given uniforms including distinctive hats to proudly display their national service. Many seniors, it should be noted, are quite active and reasonably healthy. Many consider activity as a key to continued health, finding a relatively inactive retirement boring and perhaps deadly. There's a vast and growing roster of seniors who would show interest in such a program.

If seniors were deployed abroad, the system would call for the foreign country to take care of all expenses – food, accommodations, local transportation, et al. The foreign nation would also be responsible for medical care, but up to a point. If the senior were diagnosed to need more specialized medical care of any kind, the U.S. would pick up the cost of transportation either back here or to another designated medical center. If a senior had the misfortune to die abroad, the U.S. would also be responsible for repatriation of the remains.

Each senior would sign a contract to cover a two-year period, which could then be extended annually for one-year segments.

As long as seniors were abroad, there might be a corresponding deduction in their payments for Medicare coverage, but this would have to be worked out. The savings to the U.S. could be significant. But such seniors would continue to receive all due Social Security payments.

Participating seniors would be modesty paid for their services. Escrow interest bearing accounts, if desired, could be set up for those living abroad

It's problematical how such a program would fare with Congress. It would seem approval would come over any savings on the health care front for seniors stationed overseas, but programs affecting seniors – and their votes – generate strong concerns from all quarters. The Bush attempt to let seniors invest a portion of their pay for stock market investment was squashed. However, such a monumental national dialogue is clearly needed as the numbers of the old mount.

Several foreign countries, primarily those considered less developed, might well look with favor on the program to the extent that their budgets allowed. In that instance, they might well ask that the U.S. provide considerable subsidization.

Nothing ventured, nothing gained – except significance utilization of a growing American resource.

37 - Plea Bargaining Club

Many aspects of the American lifestyle and ethos have spawned all sorts of clubs, conspiracies, and claims. Several have received little if any exposure. With the great number of high-level court cases completed, underway and anticipated, there is little surprise that a new social organization is under consideration - the Plea Bargaining Club of America.

Predictably, such a club would bring about strong opinions, pro and con, from legal circles as well as the general public.

Plea bargaining is hardly new. People accused of various crimes accept lesser sentences in exchange for furnishing information to prosecutors who can then use this information to net higher game, or simply to ring up another "win" in their records and their chances to ascend the political hierarchy.

It's likely the club might not have come about if it weren't for all the scandals like Watergate, Iran-Contra, Abu Ghraib, Scooter Libby, Enron, and many other situations and dubious personalities. A small forest would have to be torn down to provide sufficient paper to record every plea bargain in American courts.

One obvious benefit of such a club would be in educating the American people more about our legal system. To some extent, all these high level cases have given plea bargaining a bad name to some extent. People may think it's more often than not some sort of shady manipulation that's available only to VIPs who can afford high-priced lawyers. But the truth of the matter is that many criminals of lesser notoriety are offered and often take plea bargains to avoid jail time or gain reduced jail time.

Qualifications for membership would be simple. All one would have to do is get a lesser charge than the one originally charged with, and it can be anything from treason to far less significant violations of the law of the land. Some thought is also being given to having two types of membership: "active" members who actually received plea bargains, and associate members including defense and prosecution lawyers, and perhaps judges, too.

Under its suggested charter, the PBC would be a social club with its headquarters in Washington D.C. but with branches in other major cities. However, it would accept its educational responsibilities to explain and uphold the finest traditions of American jurisprudence, which includes the useful practice of plea bargaining. A good deal of collateral material could be created and disseminated.

The club could also offer various public services such as a speaker's bureau. Members could talk at universities and law schools as well as before fraternal and social clubs. Talks could also be scheduled at police academies. Similarly, members, drawn from those who have been involved in plea bargaining – both the accused as well as defense and prosecution lawyers - can readily illuminate the means and methods that come into play in plea bargaining tactics. How accurate are the many such sessions shown in movies and television shows? Useful brochures, detailing how plea bargaining advances the cause of justice and saves on incarceration costs, can enhance public knowledge and decrease the stigma that sometimes attaches to the procedure.

Members will be allowed, as current thought goes, to be paid for their speeches. In the same vein, they'll be allowed to write books and even see their literary output turned into films and television fare. Some modification might be needed on any laws prohibiting a criminal from profiting from their crimes. Perhaps some balance can be drawn between personal and public benefit from a criminal writing a best seller or landing a lucrative sale of the book to film producers. Undoubtedly, a liberal policy on this score could help released prisoners get a foothold in society after their incarceration while also reducing the rate of recidivism.

A strong public relations campaign would doubtless precede formation of such a club to forestall any negative images and connotations. These impressions might include that such a club is just for people who have gotten off on lesser charges, while possibly ratting out on others. Plea bargaining, opponents might argue, puts a premium on beating the system and hardly honors our legal system.

Supporters are likely to counter that plea bargaining helps the prosecution get convictions, clears our overworked courts of many cases, and helps to avoid obstruction of justice. More bad guys may get put away. One tag line, already suggested for the public relations campaign, poses the question of who would you rather see in jail, a Scooter Libby or some really hard-core criminal?

Plea bargaining is as American as apple pie, and it's about time everyone realized that. There shouldn't be any stigma attached to it. After all, it's available to everyone, from the president down.

38 - <u>SON or Stop Obesity Now</u>

Obesity of our children and the status of our overstretched armed forces are mounting crises. While our sons and daughters waddle around with their increased weight, our soldiers might face extended tours of duty abroad as we struggle to improve enlistments. One link to both emergencies deserves exploration.

There's a way to combat two surging national problems, one civil and one military.

The growing degree of obesity in children is an alarming trend. Meanwhile, the rate of enlistments – despite various inducements – in our volunteer-driven armed forces continues to drop to a worrisome point, endangering our ability to post troops abroad where called for. Note that the U.S. maintains a vast number of bases and installations around the world, and there's always a risk of another major conflict (North Korea was a recent example). Meanwhile, we have to be sure to maintain a strong domestic force to protect the homeland.

The solution is creation of a Youth Guard, a version of the National Guard. This new unit would be composed of all youths – bar none – from the ages of seven through 14. Separate male and female components would serve with rankings to be set up. One could achieve a higher rank each year, but the gradations need further thought. Under this system, the youths would be obligated to attend one month of compulsory military training each summer during school break plus weekly training sessions at their various schools. Specialized training would be given based on aptitude.

Naturally, the diets at these boot camps for youths would be designed to prevent weight gain and produce hardier bodies. Youths would be encouraged to sustain these diets during the other eleven months, with literature to bring home and show their presumably proud and probably relieved parents.

The Youth Guard, under the control of the individual states but still subject to federal call-up, would never be subject to duty overseas or any combat situation. But their presence would relieve any pressure in deploying National Guard units where most needed.

The rigors of the military training, which would be progressively more strenuous, would serve to create a far leaner number of youths. Success in meeting the standards of their military training and service would be tied to their academic work. Advancement and graduation from public to high school would be at risk with failure to keep up with the military courses and training. One key factor would be weekly weight sessions under the banner of SON or Stop Obesity Now. Youths whose weight exceeded the norm set for their age and height would receive a failing grade and face remedial assignments until they attained the correct weight. Exceptions could be made for valid medical reasons.

At the end of the seven-year period, the youths could opt to continue their military service by enlisting, attending college under a ROTC program, or joining the National Guard in their state. Many, it is hoped, would opt to choose a military career. Regardless, their bodies would be fitter.

Critics of these twin programs are likely to compare the military aspect to what the Nazis did with German youths, and charge the U.S. would become some sort of militaristic, neo-fascist state. Some observers might even go much further back in history and liken this weight-oriented military program to the severe training male youths in ancient Sparta received starting at the age of seven, when they were actually taken away from their parents. But the American students would still live at home, except for summer training at special boot camps.

The bottom line is that adoption of the SON program would help the U.S. to have a better number of militarily trained, hardy, and non-obese youths.

SON may be upon us soon, and the sooner the better!

39 - Mandatory Bicycle Use

More creative thinking has to be applied to energy problems. No matter how much we reduce our need for oil, or manage to produce our own through off-shore drilling, we're still dependent on fossil fuels. This situation will only increase as the population expands. Solar heating is helpful, and so is natural gas, but there's another aid that can easily be applied if the government stands behind it.

Bicycles!

Consider the advantages. Suppose a law was passed that everyone under the age of, say fifty, had to use a bicycle in going to work or for any errand if the distance to be traversed was less than one mile. Studies would have to determine how much energy would be saved. Adjustments could be made on distances, perhaps more where work is involved and less for other pursuits. Similarly, allowances could be made when more difficult terrain is involved and when bicycle lanes would need to be set up.

Recall the federal help given to the public with the changeover to digital television sets. Discount certificates were issued to defray the cost of the boxes needed for households who weren't otherwise equipped for the new setup. In the same vein, the government could issue discount certificates for purchase of bicycles.

Training sessions could be set up to help users who needed a refresher course in riding bicycles. Cost of any new bicycle lanes would soon be greatly offset or voided altogether by the decrease in gasoline expenditures and the wear and tear on autos. More bicycle racks at public places as well as the parking areas of office buildings would be needed.

Consider as well the obvious health advantages. In short time, we'd have a nation with people exhibiting stronger legs and leaner stomachs. Obesity would be greatly diminished. Maximum use of bicycles would decrease the amount of smog in the air, and slow down the pace of life which means less stress, heart attacks, and ulcers. Finding parking can be ameliorated in many areas. Cities might lose some revenue from unused parking meters and revenue received from various driving violations, but less automotive traffic – especially in rush hours – is well worth this potential factor. Lives would be saved from less car crashes.

Housewives can easily buy and transport groceries as they are quite likely to shop at stores less than a mile away from their homes. Libraries, movie theaters/complexes and comparable places aren't likely to be far away either. Going to work on a bicycle wouldn't demean a CEO or any high level executive. To the contrary, they would serve as an excellent role model for other members of the work force. Not to be too negative, the image of bicycle-riding executives with inflated salaries would likely take a more positive turn.

Theft of bicycles, unfortunately, would rise. However, use of bicycle locks would deter thieves. Bicycles could also have registration numbers inscribed in some fashion. This would make recovery easier. Thieves would have to deface bicycles, possibly with acid or with blunter measures, to overcome this factor.

Obviously, such a program would be a big boost for bicycle manufacturers and retail outlets. Lock makers will make out well, too. This has to be balanced, of course, with potentially less sale of cars, less purchase of gas at gas stations, and a sizeable reduction in car repairs. Hopefully, the car manufacturers won't succumb to bankruptcy again and seek a governmental bail-out paid for with taxpayer dollars. Moreover, this would be an opportunity for hard-pressed Detroit to branch out with innovations in bicycles. Again, studies can determine where the greater good lies for the nation.

Bicycles are used more in other countries, both advanced and less developed, and there is no reason we can't follow suit.

The issue comes down to enforcement. It would be very difficult to make people buy and use bicycles, especially when they're accustomed to drive several blocks to the supermarket. What's needed perhaps is to take a page from the Tea Party and steadfast opponents of any new taxes and ask folks to take a pledge to use a bicycle for their short journeys. We certainly don't need to encourage the role of snitches who might report that so and so had the audacity to use a car for a short trip.

The program would simply depend on a more concerned public accepting a two-tire policy.

40 - Predisposition Program To Combat Terrorism

As the war against terrorism is anticipated to be a very long one, measures to combat the threat while still preserving our rights and freedoms are constantly under consideration. There's one tactic – a Predisposition Program - that might be helpful though it would certainly be controversial.

Under this even more draconian proposal than the Patriot Act, children as soon as they attended school – any school, even pre-kindergarten – would be tested annually for suspect tendencies. The mandatory test, to be devised by top psychologists, would be adjusted to every grade level and continue throughout their academic years.

Results of the examination would not have any bearing on a student's grades, chances of promotion, and graduation. Moreover, teachers would not be informed of the results of the test as such findings would be highly subjective and require analysis by highly trained specialists. Moreover, such knowledge on the part of teachers could subject students to undue scrutiny. Moreover, if word of any suspect leanings were leaked and spread to fellow students, someone could be hounded unmercifully and unfairly.

However, the parents of a child arousing interest would receive attention as the most probable cause of a youthful propensity to unpatriotic sentiments which could conceivably lead to more deadly intentions and acts when maturity was reached. The annual tests could be continued through high school, college, and even graduate school and professional training such as for lawyers and doctors. Academic settings, as is well known, are constant breeding grounds for disaffection within the U.S. and to display fashionable adherence to foreign cultures and causes.

Some may argue that spotting a future jihadist in kindergarten is hopelessly remote, but the insidious ways values can be implanted in young minds can never be dismissed out of hand.

No legal liability would apply, but such students and their families could be marked for life unless such records were sealed. Given security concerns the records, however, would be available to Homeland Security personnel. Any adverse annotation shouldn't prevent someone from admission to a university, to get a job, or even to serve in the military. It shouldn't be like a credit rating. But obviously such a person, depending on the severity of suspicions, would be subject to a relatively closer watch.

Students who came under suspicion would be allowed to show redemption. Counseling would be provided. No child would be left behind due an early negative showing of a negative predisposition to the U.S., or an overly positive disposition to believe in foreign propaganda.

Clearly, such a program would meet with staunch opposition, and receiving congressional and presidential approval might be very difficult.

Some potential questions have surfaced on the fairness of the test itself, given the variables of children still growing up and forming their own minds. Others contend, however, it's at just at that formative stage that divisive tendencies should be noted.

At this point, the test would be composed of both multiple choice questions and mini-essays. One sample question, intended for eighth graders, has been bruited about as a representative query:

If you heard a neighbor say, the president was a dangerous man, what would you do?
> *(a) say nothing*
> *(b) tell your parents*
> *(c) only tell your friends*
> *(d) tell your teacher*

A sample essay posited: *Write an essay of around 500 words on whether or not Americans who travel abroad should be required to take an oath never to criticize the current president while in another country.*

The program is still being evaluated while more questions are being created for possible use. Be prepared for predisposition checks in a nervous future.

Jack Adler

41 – Of Pickpockets & Oil Magnates

Legal and sub-rosa groups alike are alarmed by the tax dodges utilized in the U.S. and abroad by the giant oil companies as well as their often obscene profits realized by these methods. Word has circulated that the pickpockets of America are extremely upset over the oil companies' "double-dipping" policies that allow them, through adroit use of business-friendly tax policies internationally and domestically, to enjoy two bites of the revenue plum.

The consternation does have a semantic matrix. The word "dip" has a connotation with pickpockets practicing their trade. Their core argument is that while they're crooks they're not in the same league with the Washington crowd, often more intent on reelection than in serving the public, and the greedy oil companies which concentrate on ever higher profits and dividends to stock holders. While it may seem ironic, they protest – albeit silently to date – to being connected in any way to a well-heeled element that might, in their own way, be susceptible to dubious practices.

It boils down to an allegation that they pick one pocket at a time while oil magnates and politicians pick everyone's pocket.

Pickpockets also cite that they're just small businessmen. They don't operate in multinational cartels, and get tax breaks from the U.S. and foreign countries. Without contributing to political campaigns of governmental decision-makers supposed to protect the public, pickpockets feel even more marginalized than necessary due to their criminal activity.

Compounding their ire is the realization that oil company executives and politicians don't have to worry about being recognized by their victims or being caught by a cop. While some white-collar crimes are prosecuted, more often than not "guilty" parties get off altogether or with plea bargains and reduced sentences. No pickpocket, they taunt, is too big to fail. In the same vein, while pickpockets don't pay tax on their illicit earnings, this is small potatoes, they say, with the underpayments made to the IRS by many ostensibly upright citizens. Nor can they, as pickpockets, secure the help of accountants and any tax specialists.

As more than one pickpocket has stated, without staging a press conference, they also can't readily avail themselves of top legal talent. Nor can they employ a well-connected lobbyist in Washington to argue their cause. Similarly, they can't provide all expense junkets to enticing locations for politicians and their spouses, and otherwise lubricate the workings of governments to their advantage. It obviously isn't possible for them to level the slightest pressure for certain bills to be created, and others to be passed by complaisant congresses and like political bodies.

Pickpockets, oddly enough, claim to have their pride. They allege, through a spokesman, that they're not asking for any special favors, and certainly not any handouts like big banks and savings and loans have received. Nor, they maintain, are they seeking pardons or get-free cards if they're caught and jailed. Their mantra is: Which is worse, a relatively small illegality affecting one person or a huge, technically legal policy that robs millions?

With the furor growing among this economic underclass, a determined clique of pickpockets may finally take a step - without disclosing individual names - to alert the public to their indignation. Knowledge of oil companies dining at the public trough, they admit, is well known without much being done about it. This unusually select group, so the word has gone out, is considering retaining the services of a leading economist to go on the television news circuit armed with charts and statistics that purport to illustrate who's the biggest crooks of all, pickpockets or the oil executives.

42 - Philanthropy Mandate

Capitalism allows people to amass great wealth, which is fine as long as their good fortune comes from their abilities unsullied by illegal or unfair tactics. How they dispose of their riches is also their own business to a large extent, though government policy can play a big hand.

The generous philanthropic measures by such personalities as Bill Gates and Warren Buffett, two of our wealthiest men, to further medical research and other much-needed social needs, are extremely noteworthy. So much so that they should be emulated by others in their limited group of the ultra-rich.

Much political bickering has taken place over repeal of the estate tax. Such a move would mostly benefit the rich and, as a bad move, reduce the federal tax revenue.

However, a call for mandatory philanthropy – above a certain degree of wealth – makes a good deal of sense.

The cut-off point could be set at some astronomical sum, which might wind up being in the billions rather than mere millions. This would be far beyond a mere hike in taxes and closing of loopholes in the IRS code as sought by President Obama and opposed by many Republicans. Such wealth can be difficult to comprehend but at a certain point the staggering amount of money some people possess certainly isn't needed by the potential inheritors.

Any amount in a will over, say, $100 million might be automatically given to charities and legitimate causes. The wealthy decedent would, of course, choose the charities to receive any of his or her new-found wealth.

Provisions might be made to insure that virtually all of the money is used for the charity, with all administrative costs minimized.

While the nation would lose revenue through taxation, the good that could be done with the allocated funds would more than offset such a financial loss. Moreover, philanthropic gestures wouldn't need to have any morbid connotation; one could provide the donation while still alive and bask in their generosity while able to appreciate the response from a grateful people and nation – indeed the world.

Opponents of such a bill would surely argue that we can't force someone to be generous. This isn't necessarily true. Such legislation would be difficult to pass and might not survive any challenge that would no doubt extend to the Supreme Court. The question is whether the government has the guts to enact such a bill and let the chips fall where they may.

This is where the public can apply pressure on their elected representatives. This is an idea whose time has come, especially if we make it so through messages to members of Congress, use of blogs on the Internet, and other campaign components.

These donations could be put in an overall fund supervised by a private organization to make sure none of the money wound up in federal coffers or was used in any way to decrease the national deficit. Or the wealthy could, as Gates did, set up their own foundation – with their own money. Others, like Buffet, could add their contribution to Gate's foundation.

Whichever tactic is taken, the bottom line is that more money would be available for more useful purposes than a tax on inheritance. And remember the famous dictum by Andrew Carnegie, the industrialist of the late 19th century and one of the richest men of his era. After donating a great amount of his wealth for such causes as libraries and learning institutions, he opined, "The man who dies rich dies in disgrace."

Let's reduce the number of disgraceful people in the U.S.

43 – Political Scandal Fund

The oil companies have their own public relations departments scrambling to protect their good name, such as it is. Here is one secret plan under consideration.

The big oil companies have been gotten together in a different sort of merger. This one is designed to combat all the opposition to their huge profits and the tax advantages Congress has generously given them. They are going to use some of their profits to provide an annual "political depletion fund" which will be quite separate from any contributions to political campaigns or political causes. While the amount of this fund would presumably vary year from year, the theme would remain the same: to use their immense profits and high dividends to reinvest in the political system that made their growth and profitability possible.

The political depletion fund will reimburse the government all the money used each year by both the federal and state governments in regard to court cases arising from any political scandal such as lobbyist Jack Abramoff, Congressman Tom Delay, and Scooter Libby., chief of staff to former vice president, Dick Cheney. Obviously, there has been no shortage of such cases soiling the fabric of American political life and diminishing belief in the wisdom and rectitude of our leaders. No one really expects that comparable cases won't arise in the future. Millions of dollars, drawn from taxpayer money, is expended in these sorry matters. This plan has been designed to show that the oil industry, so often maligned, is a responsible member of American society and not a collection of power-hungry and profit gobbling multi-national corporations that critics often accuse it of being. Moreover, this program is totally non-partisan, even though its recognized that Republicans have been kinder to the industry. Few forget the support given the oil industry by Cheney, a Republican stalwart, while he was in office. However, Democrats have also run afoul of laws and ethics.

One caveat to this court cost subsidization program has drawn some suspicion. The depletion fund wouldn't include any litigation that arises over oil companies and claims against them. It's thought that this provision is a form of insurance by the oil companies and another means to avoid government regulation. The specter of the BP or British Petroleum disaster in the Gulf of Mexico hangs over the putative plan. BP is still heavily engrossed in the legal shake-out from its bungled search for oil in these waters, and locals from the area – as well as wildlife – continue to recuperate from the ravages of the huge oil spill.

In response, oil company spokesmen contend that overall taxpayers would be saved millions of dollars. They roundly dismiss the notion that millions of dollars could just as readily be saved if oil prices were lowered. Similarly, they dismiss the idea of simply giving the government a set amount of dollars each year to defray possible court cases of officials as tantamount to paying regular taxes.

Overall, the oil companies make it clear that the money is available, and their collective will is firm; but they seek a measure of advance recognition that their generosity will be appreciated by the government and the public. In the meantime, not to be caught short, appropriate banners, posters and other collateral material is being prepared.

Expect to see signs at gas stations extolling the plan. One tag line under consideration has a blank line for the name of the oil company but otherwise reads:

_____ is a proud participant in the oil's industry's "Political Depletion Fund. Go U.S.A."

44 - Divorce Tax?

Numbers play a role in both divorce and the financing of medical research. The numbers rise too high with the former and too low in the latter. One method to help in both arenas has received a good deal of unofficial attention.

The divorce rate keeps going up, and there is never enough money for medical research. One measure can help solve or alleviate both national problems. Here's how it would work.

Couples deciding to divorce would pay a tax on an ascending scale on an individual basis. Both the man and woman would be subject to the tax. The highest rate would be on a divorce after one year or less of marriage with the tab going down a certain amount for each subsequent year. The rate would be increased a certain amount for each child the couple had, again with the highest amount more at the earliest stage of the marriage. The tax would rise with each divorce of any individual. The more divorces an individual had, the more the tax would be on that individual as a frequent visitor to the divorce courts.

While such a tax would be another element to an already complicated tax code, the advantages outweigh the disadvantages. The tax should be simply enough to avoid or necessitate any great changes in paperwork or IRS staffing. A divorce is simply a divorce, regardless of complicated and possibly mitigating reasons.

Under a mandatory provision of such a program, the revenue derived from the divorce tax would only be used for medical research. Not a penny could be utilized for weapons or any military purpose. Or to provide financial back-up for any entitlement like Social Security or Medicare. . Moreover, each divorcee could indicate a choice for this area of revenue to be spent from a roster of medical research projects such as AIDS, heart disease, cancer, diabetes, etc.

The measure is likely to receive support from both conservative and liberal quarters and not become mired in political battles. No one is going to be pro-divorce and everyone will be glad to see more money poured into research that can save lives. But as the saying goes, the devil is in the details, and some political skirmishing can be expected on the exact tax figures in the code for divorces.

Another issue still to be resolved is whether the amount paid for having a divorce should be tax deductible, though more observers expect the tax will wind up not being deductible as that would reduce the revenue to be derived.

On a social basis, the fall-out from such a tax is difficult to judge until it's implemented. For example, how much might such a tax be as a deterrent against divorce? Would it give more couples pause before committing themselves to marriage, and even more to contemplating divorce, even with compelling reasons? Would the number of just separated couples rise to an unreasonable extent?

These are critical issues, and critics of the program rightly call for more research. However, receiving meaningful responses from both the wed and unwed might be difficult.

One way or another, the tax would be expected to have some mitigating effect on the rate of divorces, perhaps mostly with those who have a lower income. On the other hand, many observers believe such a tax might make couples more attentive to their marital vows. As the tax is gender equal, the only argument left on this score is that women might be less able to pay the amount given that their pay scale is still often lower than men even when they do the same work.

Psychologically, the consensus seems to be that most divorcees will draw some satisfaction from supporting a good cause – the war on disease.

Let's make a virtue out of a negative.

Jack Adler

45 – Dollar Insurance

The subject of inflation, which can eat away at our savings and deflate economic expansion and vitality, inspires governmental and non-governmental entities and individuals to suggest remedies. Here's one from the private quarter; namely, the insurance industry.

With inflation hurting the value of the dollar, it was inevitable for someone to come up with a way to insure the dollar's worth. Proponents argue that dollar insurance programs will mean financial security for millions living today and their heirs in the future. Not everyone's going to salt their money away in Swiss francs or buy silver and gold bullion and coins. The expectation is that many people will consider this very practical insurance as long as the cost of premiums is kept reasonably low.

Not to be morbid about the subject, but we know our mortality is limited. We don't know for sure that the dollar is going to sink in the future, and no one wants to expend their good money for such a problematical reason.

This is how such an insurance program might work. For a premium set against the value of the dollar today, buyers would get a contractual guarantee for the value of that dollar in any year desired but for that year only. Let's say, you want to set $10,000 for your retirement in 20 years but were afraid that $10,000 will only be worth $1,000 two decades from now. What the insurance program does is insure that your $10,000 will still be worth at least $10,000 in the distant future. One option under consideration is to forego cash and provide vouchers for elementary purchases (food, mortgages, cars, etc.) to reach the agreed upon amount. Chances are that most folks would, however, prefer cash.

For example, if one wanted to insure $10,000, say, for 2025, the cost would be $50 a year. Set 2010 as the starting point and the premiums for fifteen years total $750, hardly an excessive amount for the value involved. Naturally, proponents of this form of insurance claim that this tab is reasonable, considering the inflation we have now and the threat of even worse ones to come.

Insurers admit that if the dollar were to keep its value, which is doubtful, they would make a 100 per cent profit. But if, for example, the dollar in 2025 is only worth 10 per cent of its current value, they would have to shell out $9,000, $8,250 more than the cumulative premiums.

It appears to be a gamble for both sides. But insurers have the advantage of extensive economic research and well-analyzed statistical projections about currency value in future years. Certainly the dollar has taken a drubbing in recent years. Then there is the psychological factor of people getting peace of mind that they – and any heirs - won't be left high and dry if the dollar, as some pundits predict, goes completely south. Financial peace of mind, insurers contend, is well worth the requisite investment.

Questions on who would underwrite this type of insurance have quickly arisen. The answer appears to be by a consortium of Arab banks in Saudi Arabia and the Gulf States and Chinese financial interests. While there would seem to be plenty of money behind this enterprise, there is still concern that the oil-rich Middle Eastern states can run out of oil, or solar energy replaces fossil fuels; and that the Chinese economy goes into a free-fall slide.

What happens if their coffers decline? Would a default be declared, and people face being out both their premiums and left with whatever the value of the dollar might be at that time?

Wags are already spreading the comment, for what it's worth, that the money supply will always be there as the Arabs and Chinese will own everything else in this country in a decade or so and then combine their financial spread to print a new Sino-Arab dollar.

Dollar doubt seems to be on our horizon one way or another.

46 – Political Contributions Cure

Struggles to clean up the financing of political campaigns continue. Some politicians allocate more time in raising money for their campaigns and reelections than in actual governing. The Supreme Court, in its infinite wisdom, saw fit to humanize corporations so they could pour an unlimited amount of money into campaigns. All too often the candidate who spent the most was the victor in elections.

Another way to tackle this perennial problem has emerged, but it remains to be seen if the current crop of politicians will go for it.

Contributions to political campaigns will probably be with us as much as taxes and death. No matter what bills are squeezed through a reluctant Congress, ways will doubtless be found to thwart these measures and to continue the financial befouling of our elections. Money, it's clear, will always be available as long as some channels of contribution can be found. As one politician put it, "Money is the mother's milk of politics." True words!

Since this is the case, and a finite, totally enforceable bill, isn't in the foreseeable offing, the time has come to treat the problem in another fashion. To revise a famous saying, let's fight money with money. Here's how this new plan would work.

Keep the current laws going, but add one new provision: every financial contribution to a campaign, no matter by which organization, and whether made to a politician or an issue clearly identifiable with a particular candidate – would have to be matched by the same amount payable to the federal government. Large contributions by individuals would also be affected the same way over a certain cut-off amount, which is still to be determined. In this way, corporations couldn't dodge the extra amount due by shifting its contribution to one individual.

Some observers liken this putative system to the luxury tax baseball clubs have to pay when their player salaries rise over a certain point. This rule has to a debatable extent worked to keep richer clubs from excessively dominating the sport.

This second round of payments could be funneled into medical research or some other worthy cause, such as deficit reduction. Hopefully, provisions would be enacted prohibiting this fund, bound to grow, to be used for new weapons or other military expenditures.

Enforcement would be strict, with a harsh penalty for those breaking the law. Instead of a prison term, hefty fines would be imposed, quadrupling the original amount given with full knowledge such a contribution was besmirching our political system and our laws.

Would such a draconian program work?

Yes! And quickly and completely.

Will it happen?

Only a concerted effort by the public, fully disgusted and no longer dormant over the disgraceful influence of money on the political stage, will force the issue and bring about much needed change. Moreover, while there is no certainty over the matter, this legislation could change the entire nature of our current politics in which elected officials spend as much time foraging for contributions for their next campaign as they do in fulfilling their responsibilities in actually governing. PACs or Political Action Committees might be much less active without a fresh supply of money being funneled in by a constant process of solicitations such as expensive pay-for-seat dinners and such inducements.

It's more than time for political campaigns to be shortened. The shorter the campaign, the less the need to pay for an outlay for ads, commercials, mailings, et al.

Media reports on how much money a candidate, or even a possible candidate, had squirreled away would vanish. More attention would be paid to issues.

Here's another refreshing thought: It's possible we wouldn't even recognize our politics in the future.

47 - Presidential Pardons

The president has the right to pardon people in prison and convicted of crimes. Not every decision by every president has pleased everyone. President Ford's pardon of President Nixon was especially controversial, but there have been others as well, most recently President Bush's pardon of Scooter Libby, vice president Cheney's beleaguered chief of staff, over revelation of a CIA agent.

These decisions, and related ones, have led to thought being given to the creation of a National Pardon Commission. This group would have no official standing but their opinion could carry weight with any administration. Presidents wouldn't be obligated to follow the recommendations of the Commission, but chances are they would take great interest in public opinion. Presidents, it should be noted, already receive pertinent information and recommendations from the Department of Justice; but this background comes from a government agency in the president's own administration. Often the public knows little about potential pardons in advance of their consideration.

The objective would be to decrease the likelihood of a furor arising from any controversial pardon. Even if a president were about to leave office, his legacy would be affected. Presidents want to be remembered for better things than a pardon that ran counter to the national pulse.

The commission's work would go further than a mere poll on the merits of any potential pardon. The president gets a list of possible pardons to grant from the

Justice department and makes his choices. With the advent of the commission the president could be spared a good deal of grief.

The commission would have the same background facts about a potential person up for pardon. But their method of evaluation might well be different. More incisive questions might be asked those involved, and more candid answers expected. This wouldn't mean any sort of retrial or rehashing of the original situation, and the proceedings wouldn't be public. Just the findings.

Imagine what might have happened if President Ford had the benefit of such a commission as he deliberated pardoning President Nixon over the Watergate scandal. Would his explanation that the pardon was given to heal the nation have survived a commission's findings? This determination is considered doubtful, considering the furor that arose subsequently over his act of pardoning the only president who resigned from office.

President Bush I was roundly criticized for his pardoning of Caspar Weinberger, his former Secretary of Defense and five other officials for their roles in the Iran-Contra scandal.

Similarly, President Bush II's commutation of Scooter Libby's 30-month jail sentence brought about many furrowed brows. Libby was found guilty of counts of obstruction of justice, perjury and false statements over the imbroglio over revealing the cover of a CIA agent. But Bush thought he had suffered enough disgrace with being disbarred as a lawyer, and having his career in the public section besmirched. A commission finding might have changed the presidential perspective in either direction.

Perhaps the strongest example of how a commission might have saved a president, and the country, grief comes from a Democrat as president. President Clinton has taken enduring heat for his pardon of Marc Rich, who had been indicted for tax fraud and evasion, and who was living in Switzerland as a fugitive. Subsequently, word emerged that Rich's ex-wife had contributed heavily to Clinton's Presidential Library. Had Clinton gotten any hint of the clamor that arose with revelation of this inconvenient fact, he might have acted otherwise.

The commission could be composed of appointees of six history professors from major universities from around the country. The use of historians would be designed to generate a long view about the impact of any specific pardon rather than just a topical finding. Political affiliations and sympathies shouldn't come into play, though they might. Accordingly, the setup could be three Democrats and three Republicans. A tie-breaker wouldn't be needed as a tie vote would be sufficient to indicate enough problems in a pardon to affect a president's final decision.

Future history may take different shape with the findings of such a commission. Of course, we're assured of sufficient pardon cases to occupy the schedule of commission members.

48 - Pledge of Allegiance Amended

The extension of presidential powers, both sought and assumed by some contemporary presidents, has generated a great deal of controversy among legal experts and the general public. The president has seen fit, as commander-in-chief under the Constitution, to imprison enemy combatants forever without legal counsel; to wiretap the phone records of American citizens; and like acts. The power of the Executive Branch of our government has grown, and some attention has been given to this change being reflected in the Pledge of Allegiance.

Changes have been made to the Pledge of Allegiance, which was created in 1892, so this would be nothing new. "Of the United States of America" was added in 1924 and "Under God" in 1954. A little known attempt to add "born and unborn" by anti-abortion supporters was foiled.

Under the latest move to meddle with the pledge, it would have been amended to read: "I pledge allegiance to the flag of the United States of America, and to the republic for which it stands, one nation under God, and the authority of the President, the Congress, and the Courts, indivisible, with liberty and justice for all."

Administration officials, in favor of the proposal, argued that if "under God" could be added to the original pledge, so could words showing proper deference to the organs of the republic's government, namely its leader as well as the two other main pillars of governance.

Others contended that the move would be seen as another element of the drive to expand executive authority, and as a less than subtle measure of asserting a modified imperial presidency. The notion that including the Congress and the Courts diluted this charge carried little weight. After some haggling, it was accepted that the president would have to come before the two other entities if the change were to be made.

Some observers felt that setting up God and the President, even with citing of the Congress and Courts on the same level in the pledge, somehow upstaged the Lord and religious sensibilities. This overhauling of the pledge would thus upset right-wing conservatives and evangelicals who formed a major part of the Republican Party base. Many of those in the Democratic camp, however, disputed the notion that any political group had a tighter grip on the nation's theological pulse while also showing concern over any such institutionalization of presidential authority.

Educators worried that the extra length of the pledge might be a deterrent to some students being able to memorize the wording. The longer the pledge, and the more ingredients or clauses it contained, might invite more questions over its general meaning. Such queries were deemed useful to some extent, inviting an open discussion that could be regulated by teachers and utilized to further instill proper respect and loyalty to the nation.

On the other hand, it was feared that the new wording would create too great a stir with the public. Fanned by inflammatory media reports, the wording would only become another divisive force in a country already riven by sharply-drawn opposing viewpoints. People in the red states supposedly would approve the wording, while those in the blue states might not; or depending on election outcomes the pendulum could swing the other way.

Politicians and pundits alike would probably inflame more than alert the public. Many pro and con debates would follow in print and electronic media, and in classrooms across the land. Lawyers would have a field day in assessing the legal nature of any new clauses. The subject would surely eventually reach the Supreme Court, and its judgment on the matter would be decisive.

Hopefully, it wouldn't be a five to four ruling.

49 - CCEP/Concerned Citizens for Ex-Presidents

We'll soon probably have a quintet of ex-presidents, which brings to mind the issue how commercial their years out of office can be, especially given the amount of staff and security they are accorded. Just what sort of activities comport to our expectation of presidential dignity?

Here is one aspect of the budding problem under discussion in some quarters.

The question is evolving as an important issue in the 21st century as longer life spans mean more living ex-presidents. The image that our ex-presidents show to the rest of the world is critical.

One group who label themselves the CCEP, or Concerned Citizens For Ex-Presidents, are lobbying for passage of a law that sets specific requirements. Naturally, an ex-president bears a greater responsibility than the ordinary citizen. The dignity of the presidency and the country are at stake. People are increasingly disturbed by the crass selling of an ex-president's name.

There has been a considerable variety of presidential behavior after they leave office. For example, Ford, when he was alive and more active, used his name for such commercial purposes as ribbon cuttings at hotel openings. Reagan plugged a musical stage show. Carter, on the other hand, has built houses and overseen foreign elections. The elder Bush and Clinton have done valuable relief work with disasters like the tsunami in the Pacific and the earthquake in Haiti. It remains to be seen if the younger Bush will do more than clear brush from his ranch where he has spent more of his time since leaving office. Obama, who will leave the presidency at a relatively young age, will probably be quite active.

The CCEP wants to establish a level playing field and develop a useful consistency, on a non-partisan basis, that helps our national image.

Here's how the CCEP folks envision a possible bill to go before Congress

Ex-presidents would be required to submit any proposal for a commercial endorsement of any kind to the House of Representatives. The judgment of the committee assigned the responsibility of deciding whether this endorsement would be complimentary to the country, both domestically and/or internationally, would then go to the full house for an up or down vote. Its decision would be final. Ex-presidents could write books, make paid-for speeches on non-commercial subjects, and appear on television shows – but not as actors demeaning the stature of the office. They would continue to enjoy much the same range of opportunities and activities that they have now. The basic difference would be the safeguards against any ill-considered commercial participation.

Opponents of such a measure would probably argue that it goes against our free enterprise system. But supporters counter that, after all, an ex-president gets a liberal pension, secret service protection, and all sorts of benefits to maintain an affluent life style. One of the most controversial provisions of such a bill comes from whether or not to allow an ex-president to waive these benefits. This would free them to sponsor underwear, condoms and whatever commercial gigs came their way. On an economic basis, the country would rack up a considerable savings in the costs of secret service protection, especially as presidents like the rest of us tend to live longer. This aspect has to be weighed against the stigma of seeing an ex-president touting deodorants and toothpaste on the tube.

While it's not expected that an ex-president would decline such perks, there's always the possibility of being offered such stupendous sums that the offer would be hard to turn down. The CCEP doesn't want to infringe on anyone's right to earn money, but someone who has led the country, even if badly, should still have to face higher standards.

To date, congressional interest in the proposal has been tepid. More public pressure may be exerted in the future. It might also take a shocking example of presidential poor judgment. Imagine Bush II promoting Texas golf links or TexiMex cuisine on television?

50 - Political Courage Test or PCT

The emergence of political parties was not in the Constitution; nor was the domination of two political parties over the national landscape. The founding fathers didn't foresee this development. The effectiveness of the two key parties has come under greater and greater scrutiny by the public, who generally give their representatives poor marks for political courage. Now there may be a change, or at least a test.

The Political Courage Test or PCT was created as a direct response to the dilemma faced by members over voting their consciences instead of following party dictates, pandering to special interests who have contributed to their reelection war chests, or meekly following polls showing the inclinations of their constituencies. Regardless, few members of Congress are understandably in favor of such a potentially embarrassing test. The failure rate would be a national scandal.

Understandably so.

Consider the example of .the second Iraq war. Some politicians who originally voted to give former President Bush authority to launch a preemptive war against Iraq now find it difficult to admit they made a mistake. The problem, some reluctantly confess, is that they voted in favor of the war out of fear of being labeled unpatriotic, defeatist, unable to protect the U.S., and like negative labels. Being brushed with such unfavorable sentiments before their constituents, and especially prior to elections, clearly frightened and intimidated some of the politicians.

Many also feared the dread flip-flop accusation that so bedeviled Senator John Kerry during his failure in the 2004 presidential election.

Taking the PCT would be on a voluntary basis and would be open to party members on a national to municipal level. It would be up to the individual politician whether or not to reveal test results. Those that decline might offer an explanation akin to taking the Fifth Amendment and hope such a stance wouldn't impute less than a passing grade.

The actual elements of the test have been closely guarded, but some details have been leaked. Here are some of the questions:

- *Are you willing to take a stand on an issue even if it might mean losing an election?*
- *Which is more important to you, integrity or access to power and position?*
- *Are you willing to reject financial contributions from lobbyists if you disagree with their requests?*
- *Are you willing to turn down junkets to avoid any obligations to your hosts?*

More fine-tuning of questions would inevitably take place to insure meaningful responses and establish a discernible political character.

As might be expected word of such a test was used by the late night comics. One comedian declared there was no need of such a test as all the politicians always voted with the courage of their convictions, once they knew what their convictions were supposed to be. Another wag quipped that finally both parties found an issue they could agree upon – and that the president should lead by being the first to the take the test.

Each party, naturally, accused the other of political cowardice. Even without the test coming into being, public opinion of politicians – never too high – took a deeper plunge. Another worry was a Watergate-like break-in that could lead to embarrassing revelations for one party or even members of both parties.

Neither party, it appeared, was willing to take a risk to shore up overall respect for all politicians.

The Founding Fathers would have been astonished and mortified.

Jack Adler

51 – "Street Smarts" Course

All the political and corporate scandals have elevated the concern over cheating in the U.S. The amount of wrong-doing has even entered the subject of academic curriculums as witnessed by the following program under discussion.

Alarm over both the reported rise in much sought after high grades in American schools, and declining morality in the business and political fields, has led to "Street Smarts", an experimental program for use in grade and high schools. Colleges and universities would be excluded.

The premise of the course is that since cheating is universal, students should learn at an early age how to handle the subject. This doesn't mean they'll be encouraged to cheat, just to be more aware and not naïve.

Students will still take tests and probably still cheat from time to time in order to earn higher grades that can lead to getting into universities and other benefits. While encouraged to earn their grades, students will learn how they're creating a deficit in themselves if they do cheat. However, teachers will show students how cheating, to be effective, is done to enable them to spot key recognition features. Both the image and practicality of cheating will take a different shape as students learn the tenets of "cheating recognition." This knowledge will serve as a useful skill they'll be able to use throughout their entire life. They'll get an insight into our society not currently taught, one that will prepare them for post-graduation realities and coping with the real world. What better gift can a school impart to its students?

Teachers, of course, will need some advance instruction themselves, regardless of their personal knowledge about the subject. Parents, naturally, would be advised of the new course which wouldn't have to be mandatory. It's expected, nonetheless, to prove popular with most students if not their parents. The class, naturally, wouldn't be eligible as an AP or Advanced Placement course for college credits.

The question immediately arises on the virtue of teaching our children how one can be unethical. Wouldn't some children be inevitably led into errant ways?

The answer from program backers is that it's an elementary mistake to shove cheating under the rug and pretend it doesn't exist. Obviously it does, and children may learn this set of the facts of life sooner than many educators and parents suspect, and from less savory and non-academic channels. The trend has been for children to mature sooner in the past few decades. The rules that pertain to cheating in real life will stay the same; only children educated under this program will know the score. Therefore, they'll be able to spot cheaters, and the real crooks in our society will have a harder time succeeding.

Multinational companies bribe foreign officials, manufacturers make products with built-in obsolescence, and scams abound with thousands cheated out of their life savings every year. By showing the many outlets and methods of cheating by large and small entities – corporations to street corner chiselers - children can become savvy in a wholesome way.

It may be seem ironic at first but learning about cheating in classrooms, instead of bathrooms and hallways, will make for a more alert and responsible citizen afterward. The potential benefits to society as well as the individual will be enormous. Many backers compared street smarts to one aspect – sex - claiming that many educators and parents preferred students to learn about sex in a proper classroom with a professional teacher rather than in the streets and alleys.

Detractors counter that such institutionalized instruction will only create generations of cheaters in business and every aspect of society. Leaders in every field will become suspect. The concept of being innocent until proven guilty may be dented. Therefore, given these negative factors, wouldn't we be short-changing ourselves by such elevation of "cheating recognition" courses?

As we sadly know, there's no telling how far an effective cheater can go in our country. The bottom line, many agree, that it just wouldn't be fair to keep sending innocent kids out into the world thinking an honest person has a better chance to succeed than a cheat.

52 - Dike America

"Graceful Hills, Heroic Turrets and Merciful Mounds" are some of the names being bandied about for real estate complexes to be built overlooking vast and monumentally strong dikes protecting all American coastal areas. The plan, tentatively considered for the latter part of the 21st century, is conceived as a strategic blend of public and private interest construction. Furthermore, its proponents stress that the program would authoritatively recognize the threat of global warming and finally quiet those that still doubt the impact of this phenomenon. The lessons of Katrina and Hurricane Sandy will have finally been learned.

Far from just serving to protect major cities like New York, Miami, and San Francisco the program will, quite democratically, cover the entire coastline of continental U.S. as well as Hawaii and many parts of Alaska. Some cities, like New Orleans, will be given extra high and wide dikes.

Colorful names are favored as a means to distract the public from the realization that earlier action might have avoided such dike construction. It's felt that the dikes can become attractions that can lure tourists with tourism providing a source of revenue to offset the heavy cost of dike construction and maintenance. Severe penalties are anticipated for anyone caught writing graffiti on the dikes as thought has also been given to their esthetic value.

It's uncertainly what impact the dikes, no matter how attractive they might be viewed, will have on real estate prices for houses near or overlooking the dikes.

With greater protection from weather-related perils, small communities with stores and other services may develop in the vicinity.

Any reference to the sexual innuendo attached to the word "dike" will be especially subject to large fines. Many gay and lesbian groups have mounted a campaign to come up with a new word for these barriers against rising tides, at least as far as governmental brochures and like material. "Bulwarks" was one word suggested, but then this word was thought too hard to pronounce. One wag opined that this word could be shortened to "bullies", an image implying how the constructions presented themselves to the angry seas. But no final semantic choice has been made yet.

While the Army Corp of Engineers has been entrusted with drawing up the blueprints for erection of the dikes, and presenting a final budget, a special commission of artists has been appointed to suggest ways and means for their beautification. Murals, celebrating American history and ingenuity, are expected to grace the walls facing inland.

The plan will have to be approved by Congress, and considerable opposition is anticipated. The overall cost of the program would be enormous. Even those who realize the threat of global warming fear the price of total dike construction at coastlines will plunge the national deficit into the fiscal stratosphere. While conceived as a national program there is hope that states with coastlines will participate in the cost. However, inland states – and there are over twenty of them – don't particularly want their tax dollars spent for other states.

A proposal for a special "dike tax" on income tax forms was also questioned by representatives of inland states. As usual, the issue has been a political football, with some politicians charged with putting their electoral chances over national security.

Calls for a national plebiscite have also been suggested. Many political and even religious leaders have urged the public to stand together and handle the situation as one nation and not individual states. Chances are the costs will devolve on the coastal states with perhaps the federal government kicking in some of the needed funds.

Meanwhile, other countries with coastlines -and there aren't many inland nations - subject to the sea's mounting savagery are closely watching the American turmoil on the issue

Meanwhile, the oceans carry on their own campaigns.

53 - Arabica Television

Among the many measures to bring about a greater rapprochement between the Islamic world and the West is a new U.S.-based television channel run by American Muslims dedicated to more balanced content than found on Al-Jazeera, the Arab channel in the Middle East, and in the various Islamic countries.

American attitudes towards Arabs and Islamic culture have been troublesome and mention of a clash of civilizations only tends to make feelings even rawer. Aware of this disturbing trend, an Arab cartel now plans to follow up on the successful Arab news outlet with a new national television channel in the U.S. to be called Arabica Television. The channel would be funded and run by the Arabian-American Truth and Entertainment Company or ATEC.

The cartel believes the Islamic world can no longer depend on the existing electronic media to present Arabs and other Muslims as they really are in the 21st century. Stories and images about terrorists and jihadists around the world, including in the U.S. and Canada, must be reported. So must acts of terrorism between Sunnis and Shias, two Muslim religious factions, in various countries like Iraq and Pakistan. But the line, they maintain, is often crossed in blaming all Arabs and all Muslims with movies and television shows unfairly targeting members of Islam..

Interestingly, the new channel would follow the type of format now seen on the tube but with certain key alterations. For example, much more news and news interpretation programming will be offered to supplant what the cartel considers trivial entertainment providing inconsequential or degrading influences. The length of early morning news show will be doubled and then followed by an immediate roundtable of knowledgeable analysts from all quarters of the political spectrum. Similarly, there will be a two-hour news program during the noon hour. A movie or a series program will be shown daily leading up to the evening news. Another movie or series show will be shown during prime time with the day then capped by a late night recap of news. American-style late night talk shows featuring comedian hosts won't be part of the schedule.

The news, it was stressed, will not just present the Arab or Islamic point of view toward world affairs. Instead, the cartel promises, news reporting and interpretation will be fair and even-handed, and considerably more so than Fox News. Propaganda will be prohibited though it's recognized that some subjective points of view will always slip through. But viewers can expect much more coverage to be given to issues of critical importance to Muslims such as the situation in Palestine, American bases in Muslim lands, oil prices, economic imperialism, etc.

Series under development will be designed to show American audiences what the Arab and Islamic world is really like. Realizing the popularity of sitcoms, similar dramatic and comedic programming will be used. One of the leading programs will be called "Haroun Al-Madshid" based on a sort of Arab Archie Bunker and the "All In The Family" show. Viewers, the cartel predicts, will be pleasantly surprised to see the prejudices of the Arabs candidly displayed in real life situations.

Another program will be "Saadia," the saga of a poor girl from the Kasbah who is deserted by her western husband with her four tiny babies but who manages to bring her children up well and to conduct herself respectably while working for a profit-motivated multinational corporation and a boss who practices sexual harassment.

Mature themes – including sex-related ones - will be used. No holds will be placed on what material can be utilized. However, there will be far less attention given to the anatomy of actresses and more limitations on permissible language. On the other hand, audiences will hear some choice Arabic expressions. Translating Islamic scenarios to provide comedy to western audiences will be difficult at first, the cartel acknowledges; but eventually the nuances and subtleties of Arab humor will become appreciated. Their shows are expected to match up favorably to the current crop of soap operas.

ATEC will also offer sports programming of major American events. Viewers will also be able to watch all major Arab sports events. Camel races in Dubai and camel jumping in Yemen, it's predicted, will both prove to be very popular. Quiz shows are also being developed, with winners to receive prizes including all expense paid trips to Arab resorts.

Ultimately, a sizeable audience for Islamic fare is expected to develop. Muting will be possible, as with other television fare, but it's anticipated that Americans will welcome the availability of real alternate viewpoints and what makes the Islamic world vibrant and explosive.

54 - Expanding Commonwealth

Another way to spread or instill democracy, or some form of it, in Iraq and Afghanistan is being contemplated. If the system works, it's expected it will be used eventually in other nations that might include Somalia and Sudan in Africa and even Syria in the Middle East.

The dispiriting situations in countries around the world, with indications of progress marred by continuing if not escalating violence, has prompted some high U.S. officials identified as neo-conservatives to spring a radical solution.

As has been often claimed, the problem in both areas are much more likely to be solved by political than military means. Accordingly, this senior group has concocted a plan – under top-level security clearance – to offer both Iraq and Afghanistan as well as other troubled countries an opportunity to come under official American hegemony. This decision would be up to the country, with a plebiscite likely to take place.

If approved by both the U.S. and the individual nation, the changeover would not mean, for example, that both Iraq and Afghanistan would become states. While statehood could be a possibility in the distant future, the relationship at this point would be for them to join Puerto Rico as a self-governing commonwealth in association with the U.S.

The offer would pertain to other turbulent areas as well including Somalia and even Pakistan.

Once their political status was redefined in this fashion, then the reasoning goes that U.S. law – in all its ramifications – would prevail. While every effort would be made to respect local cultures and traditions, both areas would be subject to an infusion of American administration – and benefits. American law enforcement, too, which would obviously be the crucial factor in such a system. Domestic matters, in general, would be handled locally; but foreign affairs would be directed mostly by Washington D.C.

As far as voting in U.S. elections, the thinking currently is that too much power might come about for a Muslim bloc if they received the vote. However, everyone in such Commonwealth areas would automatically have dual citizenship and the right to bear an American passport and to serve in our military. Conversely, they would not be allowed to have their own military, though local police would naturally be enabled. They would be able to move about freely in their region as well as travel abroad.

Economically, it would be far easier to provide comprehensive support to create and sustain local industries and businesses. For example, a SBA or Small Business Administration could be set up. Providing employment for the restless youth in these countries would be a paramount value. There are too many educated youths and too few opportunities for them as things are now. The role of women would be substantially improved, both educationally, economically, and culturally.

Military control of the areas would become far more feasible once full power was given to American armed forces. Once these countries were part of the American Commonwealth, support for using the nation's personnel and money from the public would follow. In the same vein, more cooperation could be expected from locals once they were deemed to have an American identity as well as their national one. To illustrate, ridding the areas of insurgents and Taliban supporters would be easier in Afghanistan once there was no concern over trampling the rights of locals. Their sympathies would quickly drift to support their fellow "Americans" in providing long-sought for security. The same would be true, more or less, for the warlords in Somalia.

In due course, English would become as widely spoken as Arabic, Pashto and Dari and other languages. In turn, this would make communication far more efficient. Becoming "Americans" in this sense would surely help lessen the stress between Sunnis and Shias in Iraq, Pakistan and other areas.

Opponents of the plan argue that such a move might enable dissident groups to better concentrate in finding a unifying enemy in the U.S. A charge of even greater economic and cultural imperialism than now circulated would likely blossom. Fears of would-be world-domination by a greedy super-power would mount.

However, supporters throw out that greater control of Afghanistan could mean final eradication of the area's poppy fields, largest in the world, and thus lessen the insidious drug trade. Ending the divisive conflicts between Somalian warlords would create stability in that war-battered country which occupies such a strategic geographic location. The dangerous and unsettling polarity of Sunnis and Shias in nuclear-armed Pakistan might be put under control.

Moreover, the revised political status wouldn't be permanent. It could be set up, the neo-cons say, for a five- year period. Afterwards, people in the involved countries could vote whether to become independent again, retain the same status, or even become a state though the latter political status is problematical. Congressional approval, of course, would be needed for statehood to be granted.

It's recognized that this would be the first extension of U.S. jurisdiction in the Middle East/Asia. Still, the contention goes, the move would inspire more interest in our oft-stated goal of spreading American-style democratic values than our current efforts which have obviously failed.

The cry of welcome, fellows Iraqis, Afghans and Somalis, to being "Americans" may sound throughout the U.S.

55 - Political Paychecks, Sartorially

One of the reasons we don't hold politicians in high regard comes from their uncanny ability to vote themselves salary increases, often late at night and often with little media coverage. While measures to hike the minimum pay scale have been hard fought in Congress, little bickering has taken place between the Republicans and Democrats over fattening their paychecks.

Congress' sneaky approval of raises for itself has spawned many public protests by irate constituents. In the same fashion, voters have also complained mightily, but somewhat in vain, about state legislatures approving late-night salary hike votes.

Conceivably, a program to counter this nocturnal practice could encompass public officials from the federal to municipal level. Some tax hikes are effected well in the open, which doesn't lessen these officials from feathering their own nests.

Now a way may have been found by one innovative clothing manufacturer to turn a commercial profit on this situation and at the same time embarrass the politicians who voted themselves big raises while the country suffered from inflation, high energy and gas rates, and related problems. The plan is quite simple and inexpensive to set in motion.

T-shirts! Informative and tell-tale t-shirts!

These T-shirts, for warm weather use, would carry the names of politicians who voted to hike their salaries on one side and what their old and new salaries were on the other side. The front facing side might say, "I voted for my pay raise." The rear copy could just show under

"Annual Pay Raise" and "New Pay" the relevant amounts.

Of course, the t-shirts don't have to be limited to raises. They could, with the copy or lettering kept to an absolute minimum, cover their vote on anything, abortion, immigration, gun control, Afghanistan, whatever. Let's say the politician has a bad record of showing up for key votes. His t-shirt could have a big fat zero on it next to number of key votes made and missed. A t-shirt could record the number of all-expense political junkets a politician has taken. If nothing else, such t-shirts could serve to reduce absenteeism at crucial votes in Congress.

Given the impact of television and the Internet politicians might wind up with a lot of egg on their faces. Such t-shirts could have a meaningful role and impact in elections.

In this way, it's hoped that these t-shirts would keep the names, and deeds, or misdeeds, of public officials in the public eye. Some of the t-shirts may even become collectors' items, and be sold on the Internet and elsewhere. The economic and commercial aspects bear consideration.

Imagine how embarrassed a politician could be to find people walking around beaches and parks carrying prominent reminders of how they voted on crucial issues or what their annual salary was now and before. Note that the program would take in all politicians and officials regardless of their party affiliation. Fair play would be an integral part of the system. Politicians and officials could just turn around and produce favorable t-shirts about themselves.

In addition to creating a more responsive Congress, and one with a more respectful attitude toward the public, this sartorial crusade would create a voting populace that shows more interest in the political scene and less overall apathy to what passes for our leaders. It's quite possible that possession of such t-shirts might induce more people to register to vote and then actually vote. If the weather cooperated, it wouldn't be too surprising to find television cameras showing people in such t-shirts while lining up to vote; though it's quite possible those on the ballot might file a protest and probably win any court battle.

Some think the program may well revolutionize our national political scene.

After all, when you wear a man or woman's name next to your skin you're bound to think more of what the person is doing or not doing.

56 - American Madrasahs

A new proposal has surfaced to reduce the divisions between the world of Islam and the west, while shoring up American values at the same time. While this is not an easy combination, proponents feel they have latched on to a real winner that promotes stability and patriotism. On an even broader scale, the entire notion of a "clash between civilizations" may be dampened and diluted. Geopolitics and education would have a happy marriage.

Madrasahs are Islamic schools of religious learning that have been heavily criticized in western circles as only being centered on memorization of Koranic precepts and verses rather than a more rounded curriculum. No instruction, for example, is given on such subjects as history, geography, economics, et al. Showing the American genius for innovation, more well-rounded American-style Madrassahs will be introduced on a national scale.

Attendance would be compulsory at these Madrassahs, which would just be a new course rather than a separate school. All students, regardless of their religious persuasion, would have to attend. There would be severe penalties for failure to show up or to complete the course. The course will be offered in conjunction with regular high school classes for freshmen. A passing grade would be needed for graduation. Details on the length of the course and its curriculum are still being developed. Elements of instruction anticipated include a blend of world political, cultural and nondenominational religious history that goes well beyond what is currently part of school instruction.

Special emphasis will be given to American military campaigns including the wars in Iraq and Afghanistan, our involvement in other countries like Yemen and Saudi Arabia, and even our debacle in Somalia. American mistakes in its struggles in all of these areas won't be overlooked or patched over. Participants would need to write essays on what it means to be an American, the nature of patriotism, loyalty, and the role of the U.S. in the world. The Koran, the Bible, and other religious works would be discussed for common themes.

The course would also cover the history of Islam dating back to the time of Mohammed, the religion's founder and prophet. Glorious periods of Islamic history, when their culture was much more advanced than Europe, would be explored. Their successes in medicine and mathematics, as well as other subjects, would be highlighted. Critical issues such as Sharia, the Islamic code of justice; treatment of women; wearing of hijabs, head scarves and other special garb would also be subject to critical discussions.

Americans of the Islamic faith would be among the instructors. Tests would combine multiple choice as well as essay questions. One essay would be on what the student's new outlook on Islam is after taking the course.

Upon graduation, students would get a certificate to acknowledge their successful taking of the course. No student would be allowed to take the course more than once. It's felt that if someone didn't learn their lesson, figuratively and literally, with one class, more courses wouldn't make a substantive difference. This may seem harsh, but the proponents argue the provision would serve as a spur to attend, pay attention, and learn.

However, those beyond school age would also be able to attend special Madrassah-like evening courses as a form of non-mandatory adult education. Frameable certificates may also be issued to them upon successful completion of the course.

Many expect the idea to catch on with other countries with English, French and German Madrassahs to open. The impact on Islamic countries is expected to be favorable as the courses, while not full-fledged schools, obviously show interest in their customs, religion and history. Once they see how objective the course material is they may even redesign their own Madrassahs.

One small step for American education, one giant leap for world peace.

57- Military Morale Boosters

Much has been written about the declining morale of our armed forces, particularly with extra rotations of duty in Iraq and Afghanistan and the upheaval in the lives of National Guard members deployed overseas for long periods. Too many soldiers experience post traumatic mental disorders, and the rate of suicide among returning veterans is disheartening. Meanwhile, enlistments are down.

Both military and civil officials are considering measures and inducements, many financial, to counteract these serious problems while still maintaining a sense of military discipline. Some of the solutions under consideration, which have been leaked, show both imagination and different approaches by parts of our military.

For example, the Navy wants to hire Las Vegas reviews to be performed on ships on a fleet-wide basis, the Air Force wants to have topless girls see off all manned missions (drones are separate), the Army has put forth a proposal to have mobile R&R complexes with brothels near battle zones, and enlistment officers are eager to give porno movies to potential enlistees.

Opponents of these measures, both military and civil, point out that professional entertainers already perform for our service men and women so that aspect seems potentially doable on a smaller scale. The use of topless girls, while titillating for male servicemen, would only antagonize a sizeable chunk of the populace and possibly serve as adverse propaganda in more puritanical countries. While in favor of R&R, rest and recuperation periods, for our troops abroad there is a firm belief that brothels cross the line. Use of pornographic films as an enlistment inducement is similarly considered an issue that would roil the country. Moreover, critics contend that anyone joining the military for this reason isn't smart enough to wear the uniform.

The new policy of women being eligible for combat has led, not surprisingly, for consideration of what might be done for distaff members of the military.

Meanwhile, the search for what will work, and pass muster in Congress, goes on. Working separately, military and civil commissions both agree they want programs to show that we're working to reduce any more cases of brutality, rapes, covers-up, and related embarrassments including burning of copies of the Koran and urinating on dead Taliban fighters. American military personnel aren't all saints, and there have been numerous instances of rape cases and sexual harassment among other infractions.

While the U.S. often has a Status of Forces agreement in foreign counties that means our military personnel are only subject to our legal system and not local justice, the blots on our national character are still there.

Proponents say the time has come for a more realistic approach to the sex issue. Brothels would reduce incidences of rapes and sexual harassment. With more women in combat areas, and in the services overall, there would be less tension between men and women. Moreover, if the brothels were under American supervision, it would be easier to check the girls for AIDs and any venereal diseases.

No one doubts that some use of sex could spur enlistments. However, pornographic movies – even soft porn – is probably out of the question. Another possibility under consideration include a gratis copy of the Kama Sutra, though many feel this famous Hindu work on methods of sexual intercourse is too illustrative and might do more to awaken carnal appetites than anything else. Free one to three year subscriptions to such magazines as Playboy or Penthouse, or even Hustler, are also being evaluated.

A joint public relations campaign to make the public understand just how serious these morale builders can be is likely. Finding an acceptable moral line is trickier than anticipated, both commissions agree. Balancing military needs without any implication of corrupting youths is a daunting task. Nevertheless, the public needs to understand that enlistment enhancements will mean a continuance of volunteer armed forces. In addition, there has to be a recognition that as the world changes, so does the Pentagon.

Still, use of these possible military morale boosters is exploratory and none have been put through cost analysis. No one expects an easy ride through Congress with virtually any of the moves.

But the mood persists that one way or another, the morale of our fighting personnel will be strengthened – bodies and minds.

Jack Adler

58 – "Senior Day"- A Holiday Whose Time Has Come

Given the impact of demographics it's clear that the senior portion of the population is going to grow disproportionately. The number of those over 65 will increase as will the so-called "old-old" with many more people living into their eighties and nineties. Those reaching and going over the century mark will also expand.

Better health care is the primary reason for this significant change in the country's make-up.

Eventually, sooner probably more than later, there will be significant changes affecting seniors. The age when most can go on Social Security will surely rise incrementally, with seventy on the not too distant horizon. The cost of Medicare will go up while cost of living increases to Social Security may be quite modest.

Seniors will be asked to make more sacrifices, and there's nothing wrong with that. But their role and place in society should be better recognized, which is why there is a rising ferment in favor of establishing a new federal holiday: "Senior Day."

This should be a legal holiday to give it more impact.

The federal government might also issue a national senior discount card, though some observers argue that there's already a glut in discount cards. Another measure being considered is a Senior Peace Corps whereby we dispatch seniors to Third World countries. The costs of health services, however, might be thorny due to the age issue.

An annual "Senior Olympics" with more events, and one that would be highly promoted and televised, is also under review. Breaking down athletic events by age segments, however, represents a daunting task. But providing such service to the country would help defray the cost of senior recognition programs and show a strong sense of "give-back" by seniors. Certainly, some industries – such as restaurants and greeting card companies – would receive an economic bonus.

Television networks might be asked to pitch in and create shows just for seniors. Seniors could be newscasters on news program, with perhaps regular segments allocated to senior news. In the same vein, seniors could be the host of interview shows. One interview show could just focus on seniors, and there are plenty of noteworthy seniors with opinions – based on lengthy periods of experience – who could spice these programs. Instead of retiring, late night comics like Jay Leno and Dave Letterman might continue regaling viewers with their antics more focused on mature themes.

A "Visit U.S." program for foreign seniors might be created with attempts for reciprocal programs by other nations.

As many more seniors remain in the work force, often doing part time work sans insurance and other benefits accorded full-time employees, their employers may offer some token recognition. Since many bosses take their secretaries out to lunch on Secretaries Day, a non-legal holiday, it isn't too much to expect companies to offer like pleasantries on a group basis to the seniors in their employ.

Clearly, the country should do more to celebrate the role of seniors in America, who will be undergoing a sea change in coming years beyond the aging process.

"Senior Day" can celebrate any senior in our lives, but there is a growing argument that someone who just turns sixty-five may be too young to receive such recognitions. Some push for the official age to be pegged more around the old-old and perhaps the age of eighty. The perception of who is a senior, and what it means to be a senior in a changing country, will take on greater amount of public and private discussion.

But obviously no one would be stopped from showing seniors some deference on a Senior Day holiday.

A tag line has already been bruited for Senior Day: "Something to look forward to."

59 – Of Cities & Television

Television executives, keen on programming that responds quickly and dramatically to the public pulse, tend to utilize a combination of major cities and critical subjects. *Boston Legal* and *Chicago Fire* are two examples.

Here are modest candidates to expand this show categorization in a way that will appeal to even more viewers.

Pittsburgh Groceries

The plot possibilities are enormous, offering dramatic situations on practical subjects that will appeal to virtually every household. Logic clearly suggests that not everyone is embroiled in a legal situation, or has the misfortune to be hit by a fire. But everyone, or nearly everyone, shops for food and sundry items. Every household in the land would find plausibility in the plots.

Moreover, every human emotion and type of behavior can come into play. Radiant love, raw sex, rivalries for greater sales and promotion, sabotage, insuring healthy produce, customer relations, coupon use, checkout lines, et al. Health, budgets, security and a full spectrum of everyday shopping concerns provide a rich assortment of story angles.

Will the manager of the supermarket store succeed in trying to seduce the young girl working at a check-out counter? How about the head of the meat department challenging to fight the man in charge of the fruit area over whose section is cleaner for in-store prizes? Will the box boy manage to repent his small larcenies of store goods? What is the likelihood of a pair of employees being found making love in the warehouse? Who has been assigned to patrol the magazine and book section to keep underage children from looking at lurid publications?

Each week, gripping stories – some derived from daily issues covered in newspapers and news shows – can capture the behind-the-scenes drama of those in the grocery field.

Establishment of key and eminently recognizable characters would sustain the show from week to week. Envision the manager of a supermarket store determined to make his store the top producer of revenue in the chain even if he has to cut corners and take chances? Consider how his distaff assistant is secretly working to undermine his authority and pave the way for her promotion to take his place? How about the muscular and good-looking box boy trying to meet young girls as well as married women?

In essence, the grocery microcosm can provide sense-stirring problems and dilemmas in shows that will surely captivate audiences from week to week and season to season.

Milwaukee Sanitation

Similarly, competition between the stalwarts of urban sanitation can encompass many story angles. Who is overly cultivating supervisors to obtain a promotion? Who is trying to hide extracurricular and unapproved work with films and television shows? What about unauthorized ride-alongs with girlfriends and/or working girls? Who started a fight with the union representative and over what issue? How is one character handling a complaint by someone on his route?

The same characters – especially the supervisor, a man on the route, a female dispatcher, and a union representative - can appear in various shows. Each show can illuminate an aspect of their work while also depicting their personal lives.

Human personalities embroiled in disputes, rivalries and affairs will present the sanitation scene as never seen before.

Portland Zoos

Which attendants are spending more time with each other than the animals they're supposed to care for? Are handlers of snakes and amphibians taking on characteristics of their charges? Which attendant is secretly trying to teach a monkey tricks? Which attendant is taking photos of the animals to sell to commercial outlets?

Visitors would become quickly involved with the goings-on at the zoo between zoo officials and attendants over care of the animals. Similarly, the friction between zoo officials and city authorities over planned exhibits and costs, admission charges, and other budgetary considerations, would show the nitty gritty of zoo operations. What additional safeguards might be implemented to stop children from falling into animal pits?

Houston Libraries

More than football is discussed by librarians in Houston. Romances between the librarians flourish between the stacks. Erotic content is watched on the library computers while arguments rage on what books are too risqué to offer patrons. Attachments form between students, young and old, learning to use the computers. Writers try to arrange talks to hawk their books. Head librarians harangue city officials for expanded budgets to have more books.

More than quiet and sedate havens of learning and study, libraries can be shown to be hotbeds of passionate resolve and purposeful manipulation.

Omaha Museums

More goes on in museums than arranging for displays and exhibits, both on hand and otherwise. What sort of disputes go on the propriety of art work pushing the envelope on sexuality and bestiality? What sort of quid pro quo arrangements are set up to lure major exhibitions? What sort of hanky panky goes on at night when the museum closes its doors?

Promotions and passions alike come into play as the guards seek advantage, and the heads of different departments vie for prominence. Seminal issues, catapulting key museum personalities into the limelight, will portray museums as far more action-oriented than viewers ever realized.

Seattle Stores

Current events take a bow in Seattle Stores due to new legislation allowing marijuana smoking in Washington State. Who are the providers and how do they provide? Who are the users? How do the two mingle? And what's going on with the discrepancy between federal laws and this state? There are many dramatic opportunities, again wrested from the front pages.

The mix of store owners, purchasers, police, and state/city/federal officials can shed enormous light on a subject that only expand in the public eye.

Here's looking forward to a heady future season of television fare.

60 - The Verbalists-Reality As Education.

Reality-based shows seem to be all the rage on television, and the concept may now conceivably cross the line – given the perpetual need for new and more gripping programs - into a new brand of entertainment which some have likened to a contemporary and electronic version of ancient Roman gladiatorial struggles.

In one show under development, "The Verbalists," two men compete – with words – in a contest where one receives a one-time, tax-free payment of a million dollars while the loser would be obliged to serve the nation in various ways for a full year. In the program's original format the loser would be subject to a painless execution, with his body turned over for organ use and/or research. But it was felt that the public wasn't yet ready for such a bloodthirsty version to be shown on screen.

Both men, of course, would be volunteers and have to sign all the necessary waivers and participatory documents. No one would be forced to be a contestant. Solace, if any, to the loser would come from public use of his time and efforts, which was expected to catch the public's fancy. Indeed, some losers were likely to turn their defeat into book deals and other lucrative benefits. All penalties were both humane, utilitarian, and in full accordance with traditional American values.

The live show was expected to be one of the most popular shows on the air. The public will decide who was victor and who was vanquished between a pair of contestants often referred to as *verbalists*. Harsher adversarial contests, featuring lithe youthful contestants performing arduous physical tasks in exotic locations, had lost some of their luster. Finally there was a show which appealed, as the producer's press release boasted, to the finer angels of the American viewing public.

The educative value, which some had initially mocked, was now recognized as sound. It was well-known and recognized now that many viewers, especially younger ones still perhaps in school or those seeking to make their way in the world, would profit from the knowledge disseminated in the weekly programs. No one, it was anticipated by the show's producers, would impugn the level of academic excellence expected to be exhibited in each show. Many industry observers noted that the show lacked any lurid sex overtones or overt violence and was thus well suited for prime time viewing.

Indeed, initial screening for contestants would be stringent, with many expected to fail. *The Verbalists,* the producers were sure, would be accepted as cutting edge public entertainment. High ratings would surely be established quickly and then sustained. Having a winner and loser, with both facing either the reward or the penalty, would give the show more bite than just ladling out money to one person.

Each show would feature a word theme that the contestants would have to respond to. Their answers would be electronically scored by the show and a live audience. Even the selection of the word "taunts" instead of the more vulgar "insults" displayed how the show's impressive pedagogical character would be highlighted in the pilot show being readied. But the specifics of the penalty would be withheld from the contestants, the live studio audience, and the viewing public until the show's end and the victor was declared. However, only the studio audience could decide the victor and therefore bestow the reward upon him or her.

Once the program got underway, each contestant would get sixty seconds to hurl a taunt at the other. Viewers could both hear the single word and then see it quickly appear in large block letters under each contestant's name on the screen. As the words stayed on the screen, viewers could easily check any word's meaning in a dictionary. Moreover, home viewers would be advised to have a dictionary handy, especially if children are watching the show. A small table beside each man had a cup and pitcher of water. Small but powerful microphones would be been implanted in the armrests of each chair.

No notes would be allowed. The more erudite a contestant's taunt, the higher their score. Common words like dope and jerk would receive a low score. Words like "churl" and "rapscallion" would score much higher. But the audience will help make the final determination as to which of the contestants will become wealthy—and which will be subject to a year of federally-approved labor of some sort.

Every effort would be made to match two contestants with relatively similar backgrounds in age and education. Obviously it wouldn't do to pit a professor of English against a construction worker. Finally, it was decided that the standards of the show called for each contestant to have a college education but no graduate degrees. If one person had a professional occupation, say as a doctor or lawyer, then the other would have to also have reached that educative plateau.

The only thing holding up the program from production of a pilot show is the search for advertisers. For some reason, companies seem adverse, even when offered to match a chief executive officer against a chief executive officer.

61 - Lawyer Moratorium

Complaints about the impact of lawyers over our political arena, and the degree of litigation in society at large, are common fare. Many of our elected officials are lawyers, and their profession is widely considered to yield a stranglehold over much of the business world as well. Many dread the need for an attorney and the consequent cost.

But now a revolutionary way to curtail this pervasive influence, and the pronounced tendency to envision a legal career as a platform into politics, has been created. It remains to be seen whether the idea will have any traction.

The basic idea is create a moratorium, of say, two generations in which lawyers would be prohibited from serving in any elected capacity, municipal to federal. They could still be consultants and lobbyists. Existing laws would stay in place. Lawyers could still receive appointments to various positions.

Though there is no way to know in advance, the thought – or hope – is that we would have a less litigious society if there weren't so many lawyers making and interpreting the laws. Perhaps there would also be fewer laws, and less unnecessary complications in the laws we do need. Certainly, entry into the political arena would be affected.

Many observers, however, point out that such a plan, if approved, might hurt society more than it helps by removing such an important group of capable and bright people from government.

But supporters contend that the U.S. will never know what the impact on a slow-down in lawyer dominance of American politics might be if we don't try. Moreover, even some lawyers agree there are too many attorneys in government. Not unexpectedly the profession, overall, doesn't look upon this proposal with favor. But it's still recognized, and as more than just a saving grace, that under this plan lawyers would still be able to draft possible bills. They just wouldn't be able to vote on the laws they wanted passed and which might serve their own interests and of the special interest groups they represent.

This system, it's also argued, would encourage a lot of other professionals and people in general to start participating in politics. For example, there are already doctors and dentists and other non-lawyers in the Senate and House of Representatives on the federal level. The same is true in state, county and city governments. On the presidential level, neither Bush is a lawyer. Reagan was an actor. Eisenhower was a general, and so were a number of other presidents starting with George Washington. Carter is an engineer.

Being a lawyer isn't a requisite for being president, or running for the office as George Romney most recently proved. Still, it can't be denied that lawyers still have a head start in getting ahead in politics and in then ascending in power and position.

As a trial balloon the proposal, it's believed, was discussed by both Republicans and Democrats. However, since everyone in the group was an attorney, little follow-up emerged.

Accordingly, public support would be needed to light a fire under legislators. One idea is to gather together political luminaries who aren't lawyers to come out in favor of the proposal. Both Romney and Arnold

Schwarzenegger were considered as potential co-chairmen of a new committee.

Another thought was to use California's state initiative process to launch a trial balloon. If approved, the program would just apply to California, but then it could serve as a framework for other states and as a linchpin for a national version.

Many strange things have started in California, observers point out, and this is one that could have serious national consequences.

62 - "Create!"

Restoring American self-belief has become a bigger cause than ever before in our history. Our controversial involvements in Vietnam, Iraq and Afghanistan - and related scandals - have dampened our sense of national self-esteem. Belief in governmental verity has sunk deeply in a morass of doubt over our future and our prosperity if not stature as a nation.

Concern over the flagging American spirit, the indifference to official governmental malfeasance, and a tendency to obesity, has led many to consider what can be done to restore vigor to the national psyche. The consensus has been that the country needs a new invigorating concept to reinstill a sense of daring and self-reliance, some sort of new frontier to excite and engage people.

Now a way to confront this profound national malaise has been proposed.

In exploring the subject, it was quickly recognized that in terms of geography we conquered the west long ago while expanding the nation from ocean to ocean. Moreover, we now have an economic and often military presence around the world, so a new frontier involving land and water resources was no longer an option.

Next on the list of possible new frontiers was space. Enormous opportunities exist, more in theory than in practice – except for astronauts – for virtually all of the population. But the field is still far too remote, literally and figuratively, to allow for free-flowing creativity. Similarly, ocean floor exploration will surely grow in scope, but the field will be limited to specialists for many years.

Another option for a new frontier turned inward – the mental world of Americans. One possibility under review was to organize a national creative pool that anyone could use at any time regardless of ethnicity, religion, gender, et al. This reservoir could be dipped into through random conversations with strangers, in long-lasting and intimate relationships, and by individuals or groups. All that would be needed to initiate the moment of shared creativity and spiritual replenishment would be a national code word of "Create."

More than just a word would be involved. The concept behind the word would surely catch on, leading to a national reawakening such as this country has had before in its history.

In time, saying "Create" might even replace "Hello" as a greeting. Good will and sincerity would be generated, and hopefully transmit itself to the higher reaches of government.

On the economic front, entrepreneurs would surely spot and seize an opportunity to produce relevant t-shirts, pins, and like insignia. But the one-word designation would insure good taste in this commercial material.

Once spoken, attention will be paid to whatever that person wants to say, thus encouraging an outpouring of thoughts and convictions that would probably never be uttered otherwise. Not everyone has the talent to write books and create beautiful works of art, but the national creative pool would generate new waves of creativity from everyone. The range of opinions anticipated are expected to be impressive and to raise the national level of intelligence considerably. The entertainment world, most notably films and television, would probably show a dramatic increase in the level of material produced for public consumption.

Elements in this body of creativity would consist of everything that takes place including traditional creative aspects such as books, plays, music, and art; but it would also embrace a tremendous roster of other subjects such as politics, religion, sports, etc. Instruction about this creative program would start immediately in schools and through the media.

Teachers at every level would likely find an increasingly fresh flow of ideas, through written assignments as well as classroom work. Familial pride, from parents toward their progeny and vice versa, would never be stronger.

A surge in national spirit, as well as respect for fellow citizens in their individual drives for elemental creativity, would emerge. Democracy, it's believed, would be well served under this conceptual drive for greater creativity in everyday life.

Brave new frontier!

Jack Adler

63 - Theme Park/Balance of Payments

The balance of payments, considering our humongous national debt, is a matter of great concern mostly to economists now but the consequences can become more obvious to the public in the near future. With this view in mind, a proposal to help the cause has materialized that will help the balance of payments and yet permit the public to savor the attractions of foreign countries.

It's important to take into consideration the success of theme parks in general and then recognize the popularity of using foreign architectural themes as employed by some of the Las Vegas hotels on the Strip. Proponents of the program also reference the Cloisters in New York, Hearst Castle in California, and London Bridge in Arizona. All three rake in visitors.

The idea is to set aside one huge area in the U.S. for construction of a major park that would consist of representative elements of the top tourist destinations all over the world, from the Acropolis in Greece to the Great Wall of China. There are individual theme parks with imitations of famous attractions, but not one theme park where they're all collected together in appropriate size and scope.

Every possible measure would be taken to insure as exact a replica as possible of the attractions. Each site would have people who speak the relevant foreign language as the staff. They would, of course, still be Americans to swell our employment ranks.

The kicker is that each nation would be allotted a space proportionate to its popularity as a travel destination. France, for example, would get more space than, say, Slovakia or Albania. But each small nation would be guaranteed a minimal allotment of space. Revenue from this monumental park would be split between the U.S. and the foreign government on a sliding scale yet to be established. Preliminary studies by economists of all potential nation participants are underway.

American dollars will stay in this country that might otherwise be spent abroad. And many foreign interests would be willing to invest here, in order to compensate for any lost tourist revenue. Such a plan would also mean a lot more Visit U.S. traffic of foreigners here as well as more of our jets sold to foreign airlines.

Foreign travel would not especially suffer. Everyone could still go where and when they wanted. Moreover, visits to the park could spur interest in going to the relevant country, seeing the original attractions, and learning more about the nation.

The economy, in short, would get a tremendous boost of the program worked as expected. Foreign governments, while perhaps initially uncertain, would come to see the advantages of the program. Having the U.S. succumb to its mounting public debt would hardly help other nations, so the good of all is implicitly wrapped up in this plan.

The question of where such a gigantic park would be located stumped many supporters. A great deal of land was needed, and it had to be undeveloped land that might not be used for mineral or other resources.

After considerable thought, sections of Wyoming Montana and Idaho have emerged as leading candidates. Parts of these states are under-populated, with not that much heavy industry, and with a good deal of federal land. Natural resources would be protected as well as any existing attractions. Some eminent domain purchases might be involved. Visitors would certainly have to use our transportation system to get to this massive complex. Conceivably, some arch right-wing training centers and their arms caches might be dislodged.

Naturally, the federal government would defray the cost of relocation of people if they needed to move. Neighbor states would doubtless welcome the infusion of new blood and businesses, all coming from the same part of the country. There wouldn't be any culture shock to speak of, and there's always the patriotism factor. Appeals would be made to residents that this is a time when every American has to help with imaginative solutions to the nation' problems.

The name of the park hasn't been finalized yet. One suggestion of naming it after a native son of Wyoming, former vice president Dick Cheney, has been struck down as too controversial. Betting is now on selection of a more international name like "Financial Integrity Park" or "Currency & Courage Park."

64 - Comic Brainstorm Routings, The New CBR

Methods of combat can be non-lethal and even have elements of humor. The Pentagon, ever alert of ways to defend the country, is working on a new program that will likely astound people – and possibly amuse them, too.

Ways and means to reduce tensions between governments and leaders continue to proliferate. One new development to surface, already dubbed a humor hot-line, has comic overtones.

CBR generally refers to Chemical, Biological and Radiological Warfare, and it's a scary subject. Now an alternative meaning to these initials is under discussion, not in a military context but as a tactic to soothe national nerves between countries.

Here is some background information leaked from a former Pentagon spokesman.

Unlike its much feared namesake, this new and different CBR, which is called "Comic Brainstorm Routings", can be safely stored or shipped anywhere and its effects, if released, are never lethal. It's the world's first use of humor as a weapon for peace. Topical but amusing shows based on issues confronting the current leaders of each country would be created and made available for viewing in the respective nations. In addition, copies of roasts of our presidents would be offered to other nations along with invitations for other countries to follow suit.

It's recognized that other nations have different traditions and poking fun of national leaders not only isn't done but can be downright dangerous. Accordingly, the

Pentagon would be prepared to offer a specially trained political comedy staff to any other country. Host nations, of course, would have a full right of editing the material before it was shown here.

The whole advantage of this CBR is that each country wouldn't be embarrassed before the other people. It's a leader-to-leader program designed to achieve a humbling effect by making big wigs laugh at themselves and each other. As an example, it could work out to giving the Russians a show making fun of Obama and expect them to give us a lese majeste show about Putin.

Critics of the inchoate program contend that such reciprocity would never fly with Russia. Nor, they say, would it receive any support from any other country than possibly some in Western Europe and South America. The element of personal and national pride, as well as tradition, would doom the plan elsewhere. No one could imagine a ruler of Saudi Arabia, to illustrate, agreeing to such a tie-in.

Supporters retort that combating such tradition is very much the reason to attempt a change based on the soft approach of humor. Inroads against entrenched values in other nations can be made with carefully orchestrated material that can amuse without being offensive.

Initial feelers have been inconclusive. France reportedly thinks the idea lacks grandeur. Germany complained that it lacks dignity. China and Japan said they might consider the program but they both want some trade concessions.

Final touches are being conducted, including a tentative budget, before seeking any congressional sponsors. Many details are still classified, but the program developers assert that it will all be top-notch entertainment, professionally written and performed.

Developers are also searching for a well-known entertainer or entertainer-politician, who hasn't overly espoused any obvious political stance and who can capture the spirit of the plan, to be a non-governmental spokesman. So far the leading candidate is Arnold Schwarzenegger, who has both entertainment and political experience, and is considered by many to be a moderate Republican. Sean Penn is considered too left-wing. George Clooney is too eager for the limelight. Many professional comedians, including late night television hosts, were deemed too irreverent. But the search goes on and in a move for greater transparency the search for a name leader may be opened up for national debate.

As proponents claim, who knows how many crises and wars can be avoided through humor? Being funny is difficult, but tickling the world's funny bone can be a terrific deterrent.

65 - Supreme Court Adjustment

The Supreme Court in recent years has come under more and more scrutiny. Its highly controversial decision in the 2000 election between Bush and Gore revealed to the country just how political the court could be in its decisions. Some appointments to the high court, while ratified by the Senate, have been and remain questionable. The number of narrow five/four decisions, mirroring the political and partisan divides of the government, has created a lack of confidence in the court's judgments. Labels of a conservative versus a liberal wing isn't reassuring either.

So it isn't a great surprise to see a new measure being considered. It's time to make the Supreme Court justices more accountable.

Accountability of our elected leaders is clear but dependent on when elections are held. Accountability for non-elected officials is relatively weak if not non-existent. No one has more of a free ride than the nine justices who form our Supreme Court. They're appointed for life, so it doesn't make a difference – as far as their official status -- what they decide, or choose not to decide. Other judges in lower courts may also have a non-elected tenure but their decisions aren't like to have the impact of what the Supreme Court does or doesn't do.

The number of five to four decisions is also troubling to many who feel that the course of the nation shouldn't be dependent on the legal opinions of one justice, no matter how brilliant he or she might be. In effect, one justice might yield more influence on the country's condition and destiny than the president; who is after all subject to election or having his or her time of office end.

One proposal under consideration is to initiate a national referendum after a justice serves ten years. The referendum would be a simple affair to show the public still has confidence in the justice or not. At this point, the plan is for a simple yes or vote. "Should Justice X receive another ten years as a Supreme Court justice? Check yes or no."

Such a referendum would put the matter squarely before the public and bypass the Senate that has the constitutional responsibility of approving or not any nominations to the court put forward by the president. No campaigning of any sort would be permitted by the justice or by anyone on the justice's behalf.

With the public making the decision, political considerations would have less influence on the outcome. Moreover, a different party might be in power than the party when the justice was originally confirmed.

The reasoning behind the ten year cut-off is that a justice by that time would have produced such a body of decisions that the public could decide if he or she was excessively conservative or liberal; or, for that matter, generally incompetent, reluctant to recuse himself or herself when appropriate, and so allied or connected to political figures as to suggest undue influence. If justices knew their tenure had some limitations, their decisions might be better reasoned.

Such a referendum would also allow the public to address the balance of the court. It might be time to redress the composition of the court to match the changing make-up of the country, especially with the growth of the Hispanic and Asian-American sectors. It might be time for the court's first American of the Islamic faith.

In addition, the referendum could serve to have a modifying influence on any one court's brand of judicial activism; or, conversely, inject a spark plug in an otherwise moribund group of aging jurists.

If a justice should lose the referendum, he or she would stay on the court until a new justice is confirmed, which would happen as soon as possible and in the usual method.

The major problem foreseen for this plan is how to prevent the Supreme Court from ruling about itself. The plan, of course, would require legislation by Congress, which if passed could then be thrown out by the Supreme Court as unconstitutional.

Back to square one.

66 - New President Day/New Congress Day

We may never celebrate as many holidays as Europeans do, or have the same amount of annual vacation time, but maybe it's time to catch up. The creation of one particular new holiday seems to be gathering some steam in certain parts of the country while being reviled in other sections.

A movement has begun to establish a "New President Day" holiday, though the plan is mired in controversy.

The impetus for this holiday initially came from the desire of some to celebrate the end of the Bush/Cheney era. But there was recognition that it would clearly be impossible to get such a measure through Congress while Bush and Cheney were still in office or even afterwards. Even with a general title of "New President" there was little doubt that the intent of the act was directed against the outgoing duo whose eight years in power have generated strong support from some quarters but much unpopularity throughout the nation. Carryover can apply to President Obama and his successors.

Supporters, however, contend that every new president – regardless of which political party is involved – brings a new day to the country, and this advent deserves official recognition. This certainly seemed true with the first election of Obama, ushering in a burst of hope; and some modified hope in his successful reelection to a second term.

One argument against the notion is that another holiday would mean a loss of economic revenue. To overcome this criticism, supporters are willing to make such a holiday fall annually on Saturdays, thus significantly lessening any economic impact. Timing also generated different approaches. Should such a holiday come after elections in November but before the new president is sworn in, or after the chief executive has actually become president?

Thought has also been given to simply not making observance of the holiday mandatory, and to let each state make a determination of whether to grant government workers a day off or not if the day isn't on a weekend. Federal employees, however, under this concept would gain a day off. Opposition to this plan quickly centered on the amount of confusion that might emerge, with one state observing the holiday while another didn't. However, supporters point out that there are already national holidays where employees don't get time off.

Another point raised that observance of such a holiday might serve as an unofficial and unintentional poll on an outgoing administration. Such a development could have more of a divisive than celebratory impact on the country, opponents say, creating a situation where so-called red states celebrate or abstain, with the same process at work in blue states.

Taking a poll to ascertain public interest in such a holiday otherwise might gain many adherents. Most people would surely opt for another paid vacation day, unless of course the holiday received the Saturday option. But the major problem was deemed to be that such a poll would inevitably center around the popularity and approval rating of the outgoing president and not a gracious greeting to new presidents.

There is some sentiment as well to broaden this holiday to include advent of a new Congress.

On this score the proposal has been put aside to be reconsidered one year after a new president is installed in 2016 and well after the end of the Obama presidency. The belief is that the new president will still be on a honeymoon, so to speak, so passage of such a bill for a new holiday celebrating presidents and congresses would be less of a political statement one way or another.

Given that we provide lifetime security for ex-presidents, many feel that a way can be found to also honor former presidents in the new holiday regardless of how their records in office are perceived.

Drinking toasts are already being devised to celebrate such a holiday. One early candidate is: "Down the hatch, welcome the new batch."

Jack Adler

67 - Gerrymandering Derailed

Gerrymandering is like the weather to some extent. Everyone recognizes its non-democratic sleaze while doing little about it for the most part, though some states have undertaken measures of reform. Now another way of combating this legal sort of political theft has come about.

Something should be done, many agree, about the increase in gerrymandering – creating safe political seats by reapportioning and redrawing geographic districts to give one political party more districts in which it would win elections and thus have more representatives in state and federal legislatures. Texas has been particularly guilty of this tactic.

Despite this obvious stain on what are supposed to be contested elections, the process goes on without much overhaul in sight. A senator or congressional member – of the dominant party in that district - has to stumble pretty badly to lose an election in a district gerrymandered to be primarily Republican or Democratic.

Gerrymandering was given some impetus by a recent Supreme Court decision. Reapportioning Congressional districts based on population had been handled by state legislatures based on the national census every ten years. Now, thanks to the Supreme Court, state legislatures – which can be solidly in one political camp - can act more frequently as long as they adhere to the 1965 Voting Rights Act which means, in effect, no redistricting that damages the voting rights of any racial, ethnic, religious, or class group. Now that Act has come under

Supreme Court scrutiny. Wily politicians find ways to slip through the act's provisions.

The upshot is that little doubt is left that a candidate, Republican or Democrat, will win in that district due to it being heavily tilted toward one particular party. Party affiliation takes precedence over any real discussion of issues, any ability to choose the best candidate, and any doubt over who will prevail in the election.

Thus far, the Republicans may have gained the most from such gerrymandering; but the Democrats are trying to catch up. Overall, our system of active debate to help vote in the best people has been derailed.

What can be done?

Barring any sensible solution, such as a federal law mandating a strict computer-driven of any redistricting under the control of a non-partisan commission, here's one solution. Anytime there's a new Congressional seat, or a change in an existing seat, grant the weaker party an automatic win in the next election. This would only be for a two year period in which that district, while not getting the Congressperson they would prefer, would still have representation and a chance to sample the impact of a person from the other main party. Opposing points of views would be aired. The impact on the national political scene would be beneficial. After that two-year period elapsed, the district could return to voting in its normal pattern.

In this way, the impetus for gerrymandering for strictly political purposes would be weakened. Both parties could well benefit from such a policy. And if there were such any changes in reapportionment, the new policy would redound to the overall benefit of the country. In effect, we'd be safeguarding the integrity of our democracy. There is something intrinsically wrong with one political party having a stranglehold on a district by shaping it demographically.

Unfortunately, this is an issue the public has shown little interest in. For that reason there is a companion aspect to this proposal calling for emails seeking support to everyone listed on the last census by a provision calling for a yea or nay vote. In effect, such a use of the Internet would be like a national referendum – but only if people vote. To lighten the subject, collateral material might be developed with an iconic, cartoon-like character called Mr. Gerald Gerrymander asking people to finally retire him.

Any outpouring of opinion, favoring or opposing, gerrymandering might influence national as well as individual state legislation.

It's long overdue.

68 - Medical Globalization

Globalization can take many forms. While the great majority of these forms are economic in nature, showing the international interaction between countries and companies, there are interesting variations. A potential program of reverse globalization that involves patients and physicians has aroused considerable interest. While the major impact would be medical, there are economic values involved as well, especially for budget-conscious patients who may need a certain operation but are leery of the high cost, even with insurance.

Many advocates now believe it's time for reverse medical globalization that clamps the flow of an increasing number of Americans, fed up with high hospital/doctor costs for major surgeries, who decamp to Southeast Asia to have their medical needs attended to in such countries as India, The Philippines, and Thailand. Even with the cost of roundtrip airfare and related logistical expenses factored in, the overall tab is still significantly less than if the operation were performed in the U.S. Throw in some exotic locales patients can experience before and after their surgeries and one can easily understand the sizeable appeal of these medical forays abroad.

The work done at these South Asian hospitals and the surgeons there has been deemed as proficient and professional as if performed at and by their American counterparts. Just less expensive.

The issue is how to reverse this flow of American patients to Southeast Asian countries.

One potential solution is to persuade these foreign physicians to come to the U.S., not to emigrate, but just to perform the medical procedure. They could be given whatever authorization was needed by the involved hospitals on a tentative basis, and then charge patients precisely what they would levy back in their own country. However, their roundtrip airfare and related costs in the U.S. would be paid for in some still to be determined financial arrangement between the patient and the federal government.

Chances are this financial agreement would probably wind up being fifty-fifty; but with the proviso that the complete tab would still have to be less than if the patients flew to Southeast Asia. The cost for the patient would still be less than if American surgeons handled the procedures. Meanwhile, the overseas surgeon would get a free U.S. stay. However, only those land costs related to the surgery would be covered. Extra time in the U.S., both before and after the surgery, would be at the physician's own tab.

The patients would be the big winners in this set-up. They would have to cough up some of the doctor's airfare and U.S.-based expenses, but with the guarantee of spending less otherwise. And they would have the convenience of more or less familiar surroundings. The foreign doctors speak English. American food in the hospitals may or may not be an extra inducement.

Airlines wouldn't be hurt as they would still reap roundtrip airfares, this time with doctors instead of patients. American doctors wouldn't be losing out as these once foreign-bound patients weren't their patients to begin with. If they opted to match the new rate they could negotiate in advance with the patient. Such competition would be welcome and again to the advantage of the consumer. There would be some outlay of funds by the federal government, but this amount can be written off as a reverse form of medical globalization. Some of the doctors from Southeast Asia would doubtless contribute to the coffers of local merchants, further decreasing the cost to Washington D.C.

Let's give this program a trial run. It may not produce much of a dent on the balance of payments, but it will probably make a lot of patients happy – and probably induce more people to have called-for surgeries in the sanctity of their own backyards and without all the detail that goes into arranging a foreign trip.

Globalization sometimes gets a bad rap. Here's a way to possibly soften its image and also give American patients a leg, so to speak, up.

69 - Journalist's Shield

From time to time the thorny issue surfaces of whether journalists should be forced to give up material they've gotten on a confidential basis to prosecutors, and there is no clear answer on the subject. Bills on the subject are still problematic and controversial. Journalists, in our free press, have to be able to dig for information and often get it by promising sources not to reveal their identity. Prosecutors want to win their cases, and put the bad guys away.

What can the country do?

It's imperative that we come up with a credible shield law that protects journalists from revealing their sources and thus a free press while still enabling prosecutors to do their job which includes bringing criminals of all stripes – from high political figures to less notable malefactors – to justice.

If journalists are allowed to make the decision on what material, if any, to be turned over to prosecutors, they'll obviously favor providing few items. The more juicy the material the more reluctance possibly to part with it. On the other hand, if prosecutors always get their often heavy-handed way, journalists would surely have to surrender all their notes and other material. Potential sources would think twice before revealing anything. The public certainly wouldn't be served.

Valid arguments can be made to support each side. Journalists have willingly gone to jail on contempt of court charges over their refusal to turn over material. Prosecutors have been known to go on fishing expeditions for material that may or may not be germane to their cases.

Some states have some sort of shield law for journalists to protect their sources. But there is no federal law.

Here's a possible solution, even if a temporary one until Congress finally gets its act in order and does something on this issue.

Clearly, someone in authority has to make a decision over what material needs to be provided in specific cases. This means that politics will inevitably rear its very ugly head. The first thought is usually to have a judge or judges render a decision, which makes sense. If the judges are appointed, then the political party in power makes the choices, which might be selections that favor their party. Even if elected judges are used for this purpose, chances are they would still have an affiliation with a political party, either Republican or Democrat, and likely have reelection on their minds.

Absolute purity is impossible, and some measure of subjectivity is virtually always an issue.

A better solution, especially in this era of globalization, is to obtain the services of judges who are much more likely to be perceived as impartial. The answer is to have Canada appoint three judges, one of whom has to be a French-speaking judge from Quebec province. The advantages are that such judges would, of course, speak English. Canada is as much a law-abiding country as the U.S. Canadian judges are likely to be quite familiar with American issues and the background of any particular case. Not only is the border between the U.S. and Canada unprotected, there is a completely free circulation of ideas and information between the two neighbors. If a need arises, the Canadian judges can be advised by American judges, but the decision from the north would be final.

Naturally, and again in the spirit of globalization, the U.S. would offer to reciprocate and provide American judges for similar issues in Canada. The system conceivably could spread to other English-speaking nations if they face the same issue of a journalist's shield. Ireland and the United Kingdom is one example; Australia and New Zealand another.

Protect the principle while achieving results. It can be the American way - with the help of Canada.

70 - American Highways In Africa

Ways to foster approval for the U.S. in the wake of foreign policy problems, which have made America increasingly unpopular in the world, are constantly being considered. One that has been deemed meritorious should be put on the fast track.

Several countries in Africa desperately need humanitarian aid such as food and medical supplies. Severe droughts take place and many people die from starvation due to failing crops. Their animals, such as cattle, also perish. There are usually a host of institutional problems in getting aid to the devastated areas. One problem is the lack of usable roads from coastal cities that often prevents or impedes help from reaching the stricken areas.

Corrupt officials can make away with money but theft would be harder with cement and steel for highways.

In the U.S. some sections of highways have roadway markings citing patrons who have contributed somehow to these arteries. Let's adopt the same system for Africa.

Entire populations of American cities can contribute to a fund to build a road or a section of a new road, or improve an existing road, in regions of African countries. Some arteries might involve several nations. As there are sister cities, let there be sister highways.

In exchange for the financial contribution, the recipient country would agree to construct roadside markings naming the American city and its efforts. In this fashion, one might in the future travel along a road in the dry Chad interior, or through the rocky terrain in the Ethiopian highlands, and see signs say, "The City of Peoria in the United States helped make this road." The actual name of the artery could be in the local language.

As it would seem odd to have American names along African roads, the agreement would just be for a twenty period. Of course, the involved country might decide to retain the signs. The enduring honor could be suitably covered and recorded in Congress. Meanwhile, the signs of course could be in more than one language.

Hopefully, these gifts would be taken on a people-to-people basis rather than as a political move by the U.S. government. Each American city would be responsible for collecting the money, which would be given on a strictly voluntary basis, and providing it to the African nation. In some cases, several cities could bundle together to fund an entire road. San Francisco and Los Angeles, to illustrate, could combine to construct a road, say, in Somalia

The thorny issue of potential corruption would be faced head-on and not buried under some dicey paperwork. American money for these projects would be kept in American hands and disbursed only as needed by an American contractor in charge of construction. This contractor would be responsible for payments to acquire relevant equipment and labor. Many local jobs would become available and provide a big boost to that country's economic situation. Indeed, such projects could be shining examples of cooperation between advanced and less developed nations.

Publicity by the U.S. in the involved African nations over the opening of a road, or road section, should also be limited to avoid giving the effort of too much of a political spin. It's quite possible, however, that the host country would orchestrate a substantial amount of media attention over the role of the American city or cities. In the U.S., of course, ample publicity would accrue to the city or cities, both on a national and local basis.

Moreover, on a soft sell basis, the U.S. government would still be seen as a benefactor. If the program is viewed as successful, it might be expanded to have cities make donations for various other infrastructure elements. Urban efforts could take in libraries and parks. Other rural projects might include highway turn-offs for photography and picnics.

There are other beneficial ways to Americanize the world than Coca Cola and McDonalds.

71 - Socialism & Communism Defanged

Socialism and communism are like two dragons of stark terror that have been dragged across the American psyche with merciless inaccuracy for many years. The much abused terms amount to politically-wired drugs that linger in minds like sacred truths, shaping convictions based on false or misleading understandings.

These misconceptions still color many minds today, and something should really be done to educate the American public, not to mention a few politicians. Both communism and socialism have significant variations which are seldom taken into account. Many people use the words as curses and imprecations, often challenging one's patriotism. Yet the related concepts have significant consequences in the stability of the world.

Communism, in its classic form, means a classless, moneyless and stateless social order with common ownership of means of production and distribution according to need. No country to date has achieved this situation, a factor rarely mentioned. Marxist-Leninist Communism, in theory, sought a revolutionary path to this kind of state. In practice, it worked out differently in the former Soviet Union, the first country that adopted this approach. But when the cold war was hot, and "communists" were suspected to have infiltrated our government, what our noble stalwarts were fearing was a state socialist country run by a dictator.

But there are other states where the economy is centrally run and one party rules the country who are not deemed so dangerous. These nations really have a kind of state socialism, which also has different definitions and brands. A country with democratic socialism like Sweden is hardly the same as China.

Yet socialism – especially the European kind – is regularly denigrated as a creeping danger to American ideals.

Accordingly, more education on these related subjects, and less loyalty pledges, are needed now. Since our educational system doesn't seem to have instructed children very well on this score – many parents are a lost cause – we should institute a method to alert people to the variations of communism and socialism so the terms are properly understood and not bandied about as baseless charges. It doesn't mean wanting an installation of any form of either communism or socialism in the United States. The educational effort should be geared just to achieve a better understanding of both political/economic theories in the context of history and present day realities.

Ironically, distribution of objective definitions on a broad public scale – at least, according to need - is part of the problem

It's basically accepted that handling this situation should be done on a federal level. One system under consideration is a mass mailing to every household listed in the last census. Some observers think this method too costly and wasteful as many people are relatively knowledgeable, if not astute, on this subject. Use of the Internet with an explanatory email sent to every known address might work, but many people would slip through. Not everyone has a computer and uses email.

Another idea brought up was to insert a brief paragraph explaining communism and socialism on the federal income tax return. As signatures are required this would show a likelihood that the person has read – not necessarily understood or absorbed– the definitions provided. But the joker here is that not everyone pays their income tax, and chances are this lot is less well versed on the subject than those who financially support the government.

Television spots during prime time, which the networks would be expected to provide as a national service, is another potential remedy. Even a sitcom came under discussion. The tentative title was 'My Communism, Your Socialism" with two equally ignorant but comical brothers sprouting nonsense at each other.

The show, many contend, couldn't be worse than the current nonsense passed around as the gospel in some quarters.

72 - Signing statements

"Signing statements" have been used by presidents to show their disposition to laws, or parts of laws, enacted by Congress and presented to them for formal signing. Presidents until Reagan had contented themselves with general statements of approval or disapproval. Subsequent presidents have issued considerably more signing statements to declare their intentions on the specific act. Powers and practices that one president assumes tends to become part of future presidential arsenals. There seems to be less presidential incentive to return to less divisive periods in our political history.

Yet presidents have limited options when presented with a bill passed by Congress for their signing. Their options are not to sign the bill which makes it become law subsequently; sign the bill into law; or veto the bill and let Congress know the reasons why. Presidential vetoes can be overcome by Congress by a two-thirds vote in each house, which generally means crossing party lines. A "pocket veto", which can't be overridden, happens when a president fails to sign a bill when Congress isn't in session.

Nowhere in the Constitution is the president given authorization to modify his acceptance of all or part of the bill. Yet presidents, most notably the second Bush, used signing statements to indicate less than full adherence to the particular bill or one or more of its provisions. This is a serious sort of cherry picking that affects the country in extremely meaningful ways.

While the president is supposed to faithfully execute the laws duly passed by Congress absent a veto, modification of the bill as it's supposed to be implemented can change everything. The full meaning and impact of the law can be imperiled. If the president chooses to conduct what some observers term an end run around Congress, he or she might be undermining our constitutional separation of powers.

Yet the public is, for the most part, blissfully unaware of this issue which has been given scant attention by media.

Finally, whispers of dismay over this anomaly, have risen to more discernible levels.

There doesn't seem to be any point to rewriting the constitution. Passing an amendment is a long and tedious process. Passing a bill prohibiting a president from any "signing statement" excesses would just allow the chief executive to pursue the same process that caused the initial problem.

The solution now being bandied about, mostly in Washington D.C. with the public hardly concerned, is for each presidential candidate to sign a solemn pledge – preferably under the glare of television rights during prime time – to never attempt in any way to modify or lessen full adherence to legislation brought to his desk for signature. Moreover, candidates would agree that violation of this pledge could be a possible cause for impeachment.

While this may seem a draconian remedy for a lesser problem, it would certainly serve as a major deterrent. Presidents are often held to what they say which can come back to haunt them. Witness Bush One's promise not to raise taxes which he felt compelled to break. He wasn't impeached, of course, but his broken promise hurt his chances for reelection.

Impeachment in this matter would probably just be a threat. But the damage to a sitting president in breaking such a pledge would be considerable. His ability to use the presidency as the proverbial bully pulpit would be negatively affected. His very integrity would be at risk, and he might well find that fellow Democrats or Republicans would not want to share a stage with him. Without doubt, if reelection were in the cards, he would face a more difficult road.

Let's make signing statements mean what they're supposed to mean.

73 - Spins, Half-Truths & Statistics
(And Don't Forget Polls)

Winston Churchill is credited with the dictum of "There are lies, damn lies, and statistics," though some other authors have been projected. Regardless, one might add "spins and half truths."

Generation after generation has grown up with only a dim appreciation of the doctored truth they often get from media and officialdom. This epidemic of flavored stories has only become more prevalent, and more invidious with the avalanche of information stemming from the 24/7 news cycle. It's not as if the public trusts media and our leaders. They don't. It's not as if the media and politicians of all stripes consistently and deliberately mislead the public – though it's true with some outlets. We're all partisan to some extent and unintended deceptions can bubble through no matter how objective we strive to be.

Exaggeration can come into play. Here's one incident involving a well-respected television news show personality. He was interviewing some luminary and asking tough questions. In return he got a comeback that showed just a touch of fire, hardly an outburst of indignation or fury. In a subsequent broadcast, this interviewer described the person's response to his question as "ballistic." Someone who saw the original show and the second one couldn't miss the obvious deception, not a major one but a deception nonetheless. However, someone who just watched the second show could get a distorted opinion of the deportment of the person interviewed, who might have an important position.

As an example of a half-truth, someone said on air, "There will be war in a hundred years." His quote, when reported by one news source, was so and so said, "There will be war."

Misleading? Very!

The choice of adjectives can easily color any report or article. In one news story someone was cited with the following question, "Where are the relevant files?" he barked. This latter adjective, and ones of similar vintage, suggest anger and impatience among other characteristics. But suppose the actual quote should have been a milder, "Where are the relevant files?" he asked.

The difference might influence an opinion, and a vote, too.

Statistics can be and are often subject to interpretations. Often whether the glass is half full or half empty can come into play. Whoever is doing the interpretation can let personal preferences swing one way or another.

The same is true to some extent with polls, which come at the public steadily during political campaigns. But it's not always established how many people were polled, where, when, from what neighborhood or place, which are all conditions that can influence answers. The number of questions, and how phrased, are seldom revealed.

What can be done to treat this epidemic?

One remedy under consideration is add a course to curriculums of schools from the early grades through high school that concentrates on spotting potential spins et al. Students could be asked to bring in examples. Such a course would surely enhance reading of newspapers and magazines, and watching of television news shows among our youth. Questions they subsequently ask their parents and teachers can only spread a more discerning perspective. If it's not too much of a stretch, such a class can contribute to more participation in the public area.

"Spins, Half-Truths & Polls" could even be the title of such a course.

Presence of such a course would, of course, serve as a brake to how stories are handled – both those assembled in haste and those gone over with editorial intent in mind. The media itself might be persuaded to do a story on the trend, and perhaps modify the use of any stray or misleading adjectives.

It would be a brave new world of focused watching, reading, and understanding of much of the material thrown at an information-weary public. We deserve as much.

74 - Ending Geographic and Linguistic Illiteracy

Take a quick quiz and mark yourself.*

- Name four countries in Europe that have more than one official language (and there are more than four)

- Which New England state doesn't have an Atlantic Ocean coastline?

- Name four nations in Central Asia other than Afghanistan whose names end in "stan" and what does "stan" mean?

- Name four landlocked countries

- Name four countries in Europe that didn't exist thirty years ago (hint: Balkans)

- Name two seas that start with the letter A in the Mediterranean Sea area

- Which South American nation has Caribbean Sea and Pacific Ocean coastlines?

- In which Central African nation is English the official language?

Tough test, maybe. Chances are few Americans would get everything right, and many would likely get a failing grade which in this case should mean more than half wrong.

Americans aren't noted for being good with either geography and languages. Even in this world-shrinking space age, many Americans still ignore worldwide geography as part of a long-standing insular attitude generated by our vast ocean-bordered homeland. Similarly, our lack of foreign language knowledge is also rooted in our former geographic isolation, unless you were in a state bordering on Mexico or French Canada.

This long-standing national perspective, it should be noted, has been substantially diminished in recent years. The age of terrorism has made America more aware of the rest of the world in no uncertain terms. But there is more to be done.

One of the more humorous comments on the subject came from Mart Twain:

In Paris they simply stared when I spoke to them in French. I never did succeed in making those idiots understand their own language.

Even airline pilots who should be more knowledgeable aren't always. One pilot, on a chat during a flight to Europe, volunteered that Finland bordered on Albania. A librarian, no less, averred that Tegucipalpa was in Japan and not the capital of Honduras. Other common mistakes: Spanish is spoken in Mexico, not Mexican; German is spoken in Austria, not Austrian; Farsi is spoken in Iran and not Arabic; and Portuguese is spoken in Brazil, not Brazilianish. Madagascar is an island nation in the Indian Ocean and not a dog breed. Turkey has Mediterranean and Black Sea coastlines, and a third if you count the Sea of Marmara.

We can do better. We need to do better, certainly befitting our leading stature in the world. When it comes to education of languages and geography, the U.S. sadly falls behind many other nations.

Several solutions have been broached as remedies. One, of course, is to insure that courses in worldwide geography and languages be enhanced in grade and high schools. It's great that more foreign languages are being taught and at earlier grades, but this just creates knowledge of that tongue and not the variety of languages around the world.

This will help prepare new generations of savvier Americans. But we need to deal with the adults of today who are the ones traveling abroad and daily revealing their ignorance about the countries they visit. While it may seem draconian, one measure under consideration is that anyone seeking a first or renewed passport would have to submit his or her answers to questions like those above. Obviously, they could look up the right answers, but they would learn in the process.

That would be a good start.

Here are the answers to the questions in this essay.

1. Switzerland leads the pack with four official languages: French, German, Italian, and the little known and spoken Romansch. Belgium features French and Flemish. Finland uses Finnish and Swedish. Spanish and Catalan are used in Spain, with Basque also spoken.

2. Vermont lacks a coast line.

3. Uzbekistan, Tajikistan, Kazakhstan and Kyrgyzstan, all formerly part of the Soviet Union, achieved independence in Central Asia." Stan" means "place of."

4. There are more than four landlocked nations, but you could start in our hemisphere with Bolivia and Paraguay in South America. Switzerland and Austria will do in Europe, but you could add Hungary, Slovakia, Czech Republic,

and Serbia. If you follow the news at all, you'd know Afghanistan is landlocked.

5. New nations include Slovakia and the Czech Republic which previously composed Czechoslovakia. Slovenia, Croatia, Serbia, Bosnia-Herzegovina and Montenegro were parts of Yugoslavia. And throw in Macedonia as well. Belarus, Ukraine, Georgia, Armenia, Azerbaijan all sprang from the Soviet Union.
6. Aegean and Adriatic Seas.

7. Colombia.

8. Belize
9.
I hope you did well. A little homework can go a long way in creating true citizens of the world.

75 - America Disarmed

The frontier is gone, but the frontier spirit lives on.

At least as far as the taste and desire for guns of various types by a considerable segment of the public.

Discussions and ditherings about tightening gun laws periodically spring up with the NRA exerting massive resistance. The Newport, Connecticut massacre certainly brought the matter up in shockingly dramatic terms, not that there weren't other horrible examples in recent years. New legislation that just tightened purchase of guns, mostly at gun shows, was defeated in Congress. A ban on assault weapons wasn't even in the bill. Kudos to the NRA which again demonstrated its fearsome hold on some politicians.

Meanwhile, a few states moved to enact their own more restrictive but eminently sensible legislation on gun sales.

No matter what federal legislation might finally be passed – and even meaningfully enforced – many rightfully doubt that any new rules and regulations will change the gun-loving mentality of true believers in the absolute right of gun ownership.

What we have to change is more the innate feelings of our gun toters than the weaponry in their homes. There are always going to be disturbed people who manage to get their hands on weapons and create disastrous shootings no matter how many armed guards are present. Shoot-outs by armed officers, and even teachers, are hardly the answer.

Arguments that bloody gun use in movies, television shows and video games create a climate of acceptable violence has a good deal of credibility. But the question remains: is prevalent respect if not reverence for weapon possession some innate American characteristic stemming from continental expansion and Manifest Destiny, or more a consequence of our values in entertainment. Or both, vaguely enmeshed? Protection of homes and person or sport? This is another key issue. Both deserve consideration.

A program to temper a propensity to have guns needs to break down this duality. People have a reasonable right to have a gun handy to protect themselves and their households. This is especially true in rural areas and states where gun ownership is common; and their viewpoint should be respected. But tightening the provisions governing gun sales isn't going to take away their right to gun ownership. This is a bogus issue promoted by the NRA.

The impetus for gun ownership is less true in cities, even in neighborhoods where crime is rampant. Guns per se don't deter crime; they promote it. Putting guns in the hands of teachers and school personnel is more a recipe for disaster than a deterrent and protective measure.

The facile NRA mantra that only a good guy with a gun can handle a bad guy with a gun is blatantly false.

Decreasing the desire for possession of guns for sport should be the national focus.

In this regard, one potential remedy – sure to be strongly resisted – would be to modify hunting periods. Whatever vicarious enjoyment comes from killing wild animals and birds should be sacrificed to lessening the profusion of weapons, especially assault weapons that hardly seem sporting. If any culling of wild animals is needed due to over population, the federal/state governments can get it done.

Possibly, fishing can serve to satisfy the urge to show control over creatures of the wild and provide food as well. Consider as well the dietary advantages of ending hunting as we know it. People would eat less red meat, have lower cholesterol levels, be less obese, and live longer. Fish, by and large, are a good component of a healthy diet.

Another measure is simply education that should start at an early age, probably in grade school, and then be sustained in high school. Establish a course, perhaps as an adjunct to history classes, which goes over the history of guns to the present. Gruesome as it might sound vivid films that show the destructive capacity of various weapons might instill an aversion to guns rather than an affinity. We'll never know if we don't try. Keep in mind that our soldiers have been shown films depicting the horrors of venereal diseases. This hasn't prevented soldiers from contracting such maladies but it probably has decreased the incidence.

The controversy over the meaning of the second amendment and the right to bear arms has continued despite the Supreme Court's ruling on the issue. This ongoing debate will lose its steam once our love affair with guns is less robust for the sports-minded. To provide an outlet for this denied affection another idea has sprung up: instead of shooting ranges, Coney Island and carnival like shooting arcades should be spread around cities.

Markmanship will be maintained with less unintended lethal consequences. Rather than trinkets of one kind or another, the real prize of less overall violence will be realized by all the patrons of the shooting arcades as well as the general public.

Slogans are being developed to advance this cause. The most popular one to date, already slated to be on t-shirts, is: "Shoot less, love more."

76 - School For Benign Dictators

The U.S. provides training of various sorts for the military and law enforcement personnel of foreign countries. Such training usually devolves into protecting the status of the involved governments. Alarmingly, these men and women from abroad aren't studying, for the most part, institution of democratic features in their homelands.

The U.S., on the other hand, has stated quite clearly that it favors the spread of democracy around the world. The lack of consistency between what we profess to be our values and our practice of supporting various dictatorships has been well noted. We bolstered some dictators because they provided bulwarks against the spread of what we considered communism, believed to be the worst of the two evils. Sustaining economic dominance was surely another favor. The notion often thrown out about certain despots was, "He's a bastard, but he's our bastard!"

So it's time for practical realism in order that we never again be castigated for propping up dictators. Since we will for various reasons of policy support dictators, let's improve the quality of these power-hungry men and women. Cries have accordingly emerged for a new school to train benign dictators.

Promising candidates from countries subject to such one person/one party rule can send their best and brightest to us when they're young and able to fully understand principles of benign dictatorship.

The intensive and hands-on curriculum can explore ways that the American experience can be initiated into foreign cultures which have no background in our form of pluralistic government. Realism will be at the core of each course. Every effort will be made to instill understanding and methodology of achieving a meaningful, even if painfully slow, transplantation of our values.

Case histories will be dissected, both successes and failures. Students will see what worked in post World War II Germany and Japan and what caused failures in other countries.

Every facet of how crucial political, economic and cultural institutions, the very building blocks of representative democratic governance, will be broken down and analyzed. While the courses will be at the school's location, with no expense spared to make it a first-rate learning institution, certain field trips will take place so that students can see the fabric of our society in action and not just in theory.

The perils of family dynasties, excessive central control of economies, and using a frightening security apparatus will be unflinchingly covered. In the same vein, the dangers of secret foreign bank accounts, and amassing personal wealth, will be discussed in revealing and unfaltering detail.

Instructors will be both American and foreign. Teachers from Islamic countries will be on the faculty to explore how religion and politics merge in Islamic values and how this relationship affects the liberties we in the west take for granted as well as international relations. The built-in perils of handing over controls of a nation on an oligarchic basis will be highlighted. At least one mullah, probably an exiled one, will come from Iran to discuss the roots of a theocratic dictatorship.

Criticism of the U.S. will not only be tolerated, it will be expected. Land grabs, Indian subjugation, economic colonialism, and the whole bag of the sorrier episodes of our less than perfect history, will be dissected. One supporter of the putative school has even suggested a sign be posted in each classroom: "We're not perfect!"

It's expected that each graduate, upon returning to his own country, will be able to – if circumstances permit and he is called upon – to exert total control in a way that while dictatorial still benefits his nation, his neighbors, and the entire world.

To judge the success of the American School for Benign Dictators may take a generation or two, but the expenditure will be worth the effort. Hope exists that comparable institutions will eventually spring up in other nations like Great Britain and France.

As is usually the case, one of the factors in such a judgment, premature as it may be, is the element of imitation being the sincerest form of flattery. In this instance, with unintended flattery, there are reports of a School for Disallusioned Western Leaders being planned for Mecca and Teheran.

77 - Ban Bullets, Not Guns

Aristophanes, the ancient Athens dramatist, wrote a satiric play, *Lyistrata*, where wives got together and withheld sex from their warrior husbands during the Peloponnesian War until they put an end to fighting and war.

A contemporary remedy wouldn't work of course, but the premise of withholding something a lot less sexier might solve the gun impasse.

Ban bullets, not guns. Or, to the contrary, only allow dummy bullets to be sold to the public, with real bullets reserved for law enforcement and military personnel.

Either or both policies would contribute to creating a revolutionary stoppage to the rash of shootings that plague the country, How it would affect the struggle between proponents of anti-gun legislation and the fervent subscribers to the Second Amendment is uncertain. Lawyers could have a field day arguing how bullets come into play in the amendment's meaning. There's no doubt, however, that there would be an underground market for real bullets.

The worldwide reputation of the U.S. as a nation of mental cases with easy access to military-style assault weapons would plummet. Our embarrassingly high ranking among countries for the number of gun-related deaths would similarly fall.

Under a ban of lethal bullets the public at large would be rationed for how many they could get during a stipulated period. More bullets might be allocated to people in rural areas, with the understanding that they might have a greater need outside of sport killing. But everyone would get a certain amount of bullets, with no discrimination. However, everyone who received a bullet ration would have to pass a review to weed out weirdos and possible miscreants. This task would be entrusted to local police departments. Anyone not willing to be so registered would be denied bullets. The NRA would put up with a stink, but perhaps it would finally lose a battle. One can always hope.

How many bullets to provide people, on possibly a quarterly basis, would depend on a critical study. It's expected, however, that the public would quickly adjust to these changes in whatever way they're implemented.

Very much on the plus side, both sides of the bitter struggle over gun possession would get something out of these much needed compromises.

Bullet manufacturers would still be able to maintain their productive facilities. The supply of bullets, while federally controlled, could be sold out on a subcontractual basis by all the gun stores. They would lose some business but the government might provide a subsidy just as it did with corn growers and digital television sets, etc.

People would still be able to sell and trade their allotment of bullets.

Moreover, shooting ranges would continue in operation, using the same non-lethal bullets now in operation.

Many observers prefer only supplying dummy bullets to the public except in relatively isolated cases, generally for people in rural areas. While they can still be harmful, and possibly even lethal, chances are they would still dramatically reduce the number of weapon misuse. Indeed, rationing can also be a factor with dummy bullets.

Consider the potential mental effect of bullets that don't rip bodies apart. Would dummy bullets still hold the same appeal for sick minds burdened with the twisted desire to kill innocent people at random? Probably not. Whatever thrill and satisfaction that such tortured minds felt from inflicting wholesale horror would be greatly vitiated. On the other hand, it's felt there would be less of a sense of empowerment for people, especially disgruntled teenagers who haven't learned or can't learn how to muzzle their harmful instincts, in realizing that what they hold in their hands isn't as potent as before. Studies, however, would have to be made.

There would be no danger of children finding loaded weapons in their homes and tragically using them on themselves and others.

Note that both programs do nothing to lessen the love affair Americans have with their guns. Guns would continue to be sold. While it would be preferable to prohibit sale of military-style assault weapons, and at least to limit their clips, private collections would remain intact. Shooting ranges would function and so would gun shows. Gun play in entertainment shows would still be plentiful and the flow of blood unabated.

The only thing that would change is the incidence of needless deaths and casualties. Who would be the dummies then?

78 - Corporate Luxury Tax On Excessive Salaries

Major League baseball applies a luxury tax on teams whose combined player salaries go over a certain amount. This policy is designed, among other factors, to stop richer teams for securing the best players. The program is far from successful as rich teams – the New York Yankees and more recently the Los Angeles Dodgers – just pay the luxury tax and continue to sign better players in the marketplace.

As the starting salary for players has reached astounding levels, and top players sign contracts for millions of dollars a year (with playing time about eight or nine months of the year), an enormous amount of money is involved. However, the extra money teams spend that exceed salary levels is put to good use by the baseball authorities.

Social critics are now calling for the same principle to be applied to the astronomical salaries of corporate presidents and chief operating officers. Once top salaries reach a certain point, why shouldn't corporations be required to pay a corporate luxury tax, in this case to the federal government? This wouldn't be a tax in the normal sense of the word, and it certainly shouldn't be deductible.

All the money gathered in this process could be used for medical research on different diseases like cancer and diabetes.

As the money to pay these top executives is obviously available the net worth of these corporations wouldn't suffer. Nor would potential dividends be negatively affected to the extent of souring the stock market, etc. The thinking is that corporations would avoid paying such a luxury tax by keeping executive salary just below what threshold is chosen. It's difficult to believe that the life styles of these executives would be reduced in any meaningful way by loss of this extra income. Their lives and work would continue as before with no appreciable dent in the number of houses, cars and yachts they own. Actually, they would wind up paying less regular tax on their income tax returns.

Probably some limitations would have to be enacted to prevent bonuses and stock shares replacing income that would have been realized if it weren't for the luxury tax on salaries. Corporate lawyers are clever in creating such dodges and manipulations of money.

A hue and cry may ensue about diminution of the American drive for excellence and our can-do philosophy. This is surely bogus as these executives wouldn't keep their still well-paid positions unless their companies turned a profit. The incentive to excel, albeit in a corporate structure, wouldn't be diminished at all.

No one could realistically claim that class warfare or a redistribution of wealth claim was taking place. The number of affected people would be quite small. The threshold for when this different sort of a tax would go into effect isn't settled yet, but it would surely be in the seven-figure range, and at least a million dollars. Far from serving as a social leveling instrument, this money – helping to fight disease - would heighten the sense of oneness in the nation.

It's well understood that the difference between the wealthy and the rest of the population has substantially grown in the past couple of decades. The rich have certainly grown richer while the middle class has suffered or remained relatively stagnant in the economic scale; and those below the poverty level are still there. Such a corporate luxury tax, hitting salaries that stagger the imagination, would go a long way in redressing this growing imbalance.

Politics, of course, would rear its ugly head. Such a tax on top executive salaries could doubtless become in an issue in federal elections. Presumably, Republicans would be against such a tax while Democrats would favor it. But the ensuing debates, and media attention to the subject, would be a worthwhile development.

The more light shone on excessive executive salaries, the better. Let's strike a powerful blow for salary common sense.

79 - Disinformation Dissected

What is true and what isn't?

It's getting harder and harder to know, with many more wondering today than in the past.

Scandals and cover-ups by government and private figures – political, economic and cultural – can do that to a no longer completely gullible public. Deception, unfortunately, has become a common word in public perception of public policy.

However, deception – on different levels and for different reasons – is hardly a new element in worldwide affairs. Militarily, deception is certainly a tactic of warfare. Historical antecedents go back to pre-historic periods.

Probably the best known example of deliberate deception comes from the Potempkin Village, which may well be a mythical incident. Gregory Potempkin, a Minister serving Catherine II of Russia, supposedly built a fake village in the Crimea in 1787 to persuade her and her entourage, which included foreign ambassadors, that all was peaceful and prosperous in a war-ravaged area.

The Soviet Union was quite adept at a comparable deceit in the 1920's with creation of The Trust, a fake organization supposedly out to foster the overthrow of the fledgling dictatorship. Japan behaved in similar fashion in Manchuria in 1931 to fool League of Nation officials checking out Japan's takeover of the territory. Nazi Germany set out to deceive Red Cross officials when it made its Theresienstadt concentration camp look like a well-run and humane place.

Many more examples exist, and the U.S. is far from exempt.

Finally, a restive educational system is attempting to come to grips with this growingly obvious void in our collective method of assessing a rising information flow. The drive to develop a keener sense of awareness, especially in the younger generation, is paramount in this effort.

At this point, a potential academic course is considered to be more appropriate on a college level. Adult education classes would probably also be offered. However, high school teachers, especially in social science classes like history and economics, would be instructed themselves to weave in introductory commentary on disinformation techniques in their curriculums.

The college level curriculum is expected to feature the history of disinformation and include the reasons for this move and its effect on those who practiced the deception and those who were targeted. Special emphasis will be given to contemporary examples, with American undertakings of fakery stressed in an attempt to devalue the notion of American Exceptionalism. The United States has been hardly immune to a policy of deliberate deception.

Techniques of disinformation will be broken down. In showing how such instances or campaigns are structured, students and adults alike will be better versed in spotting disinformation thrust at them. Truth will take on deeper shades of meaning.

As much as the Freedom of Information Act permits, disinformation schemes – successful and otherwise - will be presented with total accuracy, with no holds barred. The Cold War period, with the fevered strivings of Soviet and American intelligence operatives concocting acts of disinformation in their struggle against each other, should provide a fascinating trove of material.

Other nations, including Russia, will be asked to supply whatever relevant material they're willing to disclose.

The end result, it's hoped, will be an electorate that can sniff out any disinformation.

The political picture may never be the same.

Jack Adler

80 - Filibuster Failure

Needful things not done, or not done completely, crown our legislative history. Case in point, the hoary filibuster rule in the Senate.

The Senate has the authority to change its rules, but seldom does. One thorny subject more than ripe for change is the venerable and much abused rule about executing a filibuster. Under this rule any senator can block a vote on a bill, which could be a vital piece of legislation; and this blockage could stand until the Senate managed to achieve an override by amassing 60 votes, or the senator yields his speaking privilege. Such partisan obstructionism has prevented legislative progress. It's also, to be fair, led to useful developments. One of the most recent incidents was a senator (Rand Paul, R-Kentucky) decrying the potential use of drones within the U.S. to delay Senate approval of a candidate to run the CIA. His declamation did get somewhat of a desired reaction from the administration, with the nominee then being approved.

In other words, majority rule – supposedly a bedrock of democracy – is thwarted to some extent. Given partisan bickering it isn't a simple task to get such a super-majority of 60 votes. Recently, bills to require checks on gun purchases at gun shows, was shot down due to the threat of a filibuster. Note that fifty-four senators voted to pass the bill. The ability of a single senator to unilaterally block or delay legislation while trying to score political points for his party and against the other party impedes the role of government.

To its credit, a limited reform was enacted by the 2013 Senate with provisions to change some procedural rules. Bills can now me more speedily brought up for debate, including confirmations of many but all presidential nominations.

However, many critics consider these changes to be too weak in correcting a huge blocking apparatus in the Senate. These "reforms" didn't tackle the key issue that allowed senators who wanted to filibuster to remain talking on the Senate floor ad nauseum. Elders and movie bucks might recall the character played by Jimmy Stewart in the film, *Mr. Smith Goes To Washington* where he lashes out at his peers in a long and spirited peroration. Nor did the changes affect the 60-vote threshold.

Under this deal between the parties both sides were guaranteed the right to offer two amendments to a bill in exchange for their restraint in impeding a bill to be heard by the Senate.

The filibuster rule, it should be noted, wasn't in the Constitution. Accordingly, the Senate established the rule in 1807 as a courtesy to senators and as a method to protect the minority from being dominated by the majority. It wasn't meant as a method to cut off debate and prevent a vote on a disliked or disputed bill unless 60 senatorial votes were secured.

But it hasn't worked that way for a long time.

It used to be that a senator would just indicate a filibuster was intended. But then the filibuster became vocal, and in a big way. Senators would declaim for hours on the iniquity of the legislation. Sometimes even days would be devoured, with food delivered and bathroom breaks at al. Meanwhile, the engines of government were somewhat throttled. Civil rights legislation in the past led to some notable filibusters.

Finally, the Senate—also in 2013—voted to abolish the filibuster for most federal judge appointments. But there's still another arcane Senate procedure called the "blue slip," whereby a senator of the nominee's home state can issue a simple paper for or against the nominee. Such a comment has been enough to prevent a hearing and thus derail a nomination.

This "traditional" procedure should also be discarded.

Since the senators won't fully reform the filibuster rule, it's up to the public to press their representatives to take action.

The notion is that any senator who intends to impede a vote on a bill through a filibuster – instead of more compromise and negotiation –should face a Senate-ordained penalty. This penalty should involve a measure of public recognition far beyond what a filibuster receives now, which generally isn't much and peters out after initial mention.

But, to date, no suitable penalty has been deemed acceptable by the full Senate which is quite protective of its own procedures. Any extra recognition given a senator might just be used to expound on the same issue.

One way or another, filibusters will eventually be curbed. There'll be less blabber and posturing and more legislative action.

Democracy, or something like it, will be fully restored.

81 – Confound Phone Marketers

Even the playing field with phone marketers.

Even if your name is on the list forbidding marketing roster, calls can still slip through this web with these annoying calls often coming at dinner time and other inopportune moments. And the Federal Trade Commission doesn't seem able to do much about it, even when you can supply the name of the presumed marketer. Of course, the marketers aren't stupid and are quite cagy about not divulging any name, the right name, or any other identifying information.

But the situation isn't hopeless to wrest some satisfaction.

Henceforth, when you're asked – as the marketer's guide sheet instructs those persons making calls – "how are you today (often the opening gambit), be "polite" and answer the person.

Here's one scenario.

"Well, I woke up with a little headache. Hasn't gone away. I was worrying about my investments. You see, maybe I should have sold some shares in Prolix Products. What's that you said?"

"Oh, well, then Aunt Sadie called. She's a real yakker. On and on. But she's family. What's that? You want to know what? Well, you asked how I was today. Then I had to walk our dog. He needs his exercise, and so do I. Boy, was he frisky. Sir, I understand this is a business call, but you did ask. Now, just let me finish. I picked up our newspaper on the driveway, and then it was time for breakfast."

The marketer should be completely flustered and frustrated by now; that is, if they haven't simply given up and hung up. Clint Eastwood, using an imaginary chair, couldn't do this better.

Finish your spiel with a reprise f the marketer is still on line, "Well, you asked. No, I'm not interested in whatever you're peddling. Take my name off the list you're working through and don't call again or I'll report to the FTC."

Fat lot of good that will do, but you never know that it might scare someone off. You could add that you'll be glad to provide more details about your life, perhaps starting with childhood.

Okay, this might not work, but here's another method. It's worth a try. It will feel good just screwing around with a hapless marketer, who probably isn't very bright or he or she wouldn't be doing this kind of work. It's the foreign language approach, but not using a readily recognized or understood tongue like Spanish. Pick a more esoteric language. You don't actually have to speak the language. Only a few expressions would suffice, and you can find key phrases on the Internet.

For example, you might try Russian, though there are many Russian speakers in the U.S. "Kuhto govareet? Skazhitieh minyeh. Vee durak?"

This just means "Who's speaking? Tell me. Are you a fool?"

But it's likely to sound more formidable to someone who doesn't know the language. Nor is anyone but a native speaker likely to deplore a questionable accent. But there are plenty of other languages. Consider Farsi, Hindi, Arabic, et al. If you speak a foreign language, use it.

Actually, you could even make up your own language, as long as it sounded like a language and not gobbledygook. Be creative. Don't overdo it. Choose relatively short words that can roll off your tongue and not seemed forced or tentative. Sound conversational. Here's an example: "Mishal, greben. Gondoom hoosh."

These words mean whatever you want them to mean. But the marketer doesn't have a clue. He or she is just going to ask if there's anyone around who speaks English, and you can respond with more made-up words. Even if your caller suspects verbal trickery, prospects of a sale won't seem very promising. You may hear a welcome click of the phone.

Try it sometimes. It may work better than you anticipate. As an element of personal, as well as societal responsibility, be prepared to strike a blow for the sanctity of home life and to thoroughly confound impudent phone marketers.

82 – Political Labelitis

Has the time come to ironically give a name, such as "labelitis", to the propensity to call someone a liberal, conservative and a number of other political descriptions and alleged affiliations? Have we come to a point, given the dreadful gridlock that permeates our government, that profligate use of these terms as political insults and defamations has badly sickened the national character?

These terms are obviously bandied about with abandon, mouthed by people at every level and position. Education often has little to do it. Words can be weapons and such terms, levied all too often with venomous intensity, are thrown at opponents like they were verbal hand grenades.

Similarly, the one word label is often accompanied by such additional commentary as "left wing liberal" and "right wing conservative." Less polite versions include "left wing Commie" and "right wing crazy" and like variations.

These terms poison individual mentalities as well as the public forum. We're all tainted by this linguistic ailment, which entrenches a poverty of expression. To some extent this verbal sickness, which can lead to a physical component such as ulcers and excessive bile, is contagious. Such taunts can become a sore point which lead to additional acrimony.

Something should be done, but public disillusionment with the general political scene forestalls any meaningful program. Various important issues invariably seem far more needful of study and action. But this is a mistake. The words we choose signify our thought processes, and the latter aren't very healthy.

Preventing wars and international strife takes priority. Cancer, heart disease, diabetes and other terrible sicknesses all deserve our attention and financial support. Detecting, ameliorating and curing mental disease - care that is often overlooked and undervalued - also needs a much greater amount of well-funded research. So it's relatively easy to ignore "labelitis." But we do so at our national and individual peril. The more we ignore the disease, the more it festers and disrupts the potential for sane and rational political discourse.

Treatments have been discussed. Just never acted upon.

One system calls for voluntary attendance at political deconstruction facilities for periods to be determined by the head of each institution. Some people might only require several hours a week, but many of our fellow Americans, imbued with self-destructive convictions, would need considerably more sessions. Such instructions, likened by some to traffic schools and located in all major cities, could be publicly funded in a partnership between states and the federal government.

Such classes, where participants can share their individual viewpoints, can lead to each person making a breakthrough in understanding how they came to fall afoul of "labelitis." At what point did such terms pop into someone's vocabulary? What was the role of parents and teachers in their formative years? What experiences or incidents did use of such terms have in their lives?

There's a great deal of digging that would probably come into play. Instruction can be individual or in a group. As with alcoholism and other addictions, some sufferers derive more value from sharing experiences with a group. Refresher sessions may be offered to those who suffer a relapse. A buddy system may well emerge and prove to be both popular and utilitarian.

Probably there would be no finite end to the class. Someone can leave whenever they want, or feel they're cured. No certificate, which would surely be rightfully considered worthless, would be issued. People could just decide themselves when they were ready to confront the political reality of the day with a new discipline and set of verbal tools.

The more the use of "liberal" and "conservative" fall into disfavor, the more our political discourse will be civil. But on a realistic basis, it's anticipated that new epithets may well emerge. The rich potential of our ever changing language can surprise everyone, and it can be a comforting factor if such new facilities offering ongoing cure sessions remain open as a public service.

83 – Political Pledges

Several Republican members of Congress have signed a pledge not to raise taxes. This pledge has been in the news a great deal, with some signers proudly insistent in expressing their commitment.

Yet these very same politicians have also been sworn in as representatives of their constituents and to serve the nation at large.

The pledges seem clearly contradictory. The first pledge would seem to restrict their ability to serve their constituents. The art of politics is compromise. But these pledges have willingly discarded a chance to compromise. Logic then indicates that anyone who has signed a pledge not to compromise isn't worthy to be in Congress. It isn't likely that any candidate for Congress ever ran on a platform guaranteeing that he or she would never compromise if elected.

The issue isn't one of principle as some might argue. Such shackled politicians can stress and defend their principles to their heart's content (and to their PACs as well). They can stand up in electoral campaigns and in Congress as well to make their arguments and voice their convictions with all the skill and passion at their command. One could attempt to sway those on the other side of the aisle in private sessions as well.

But the concept of compromise should never be lost. The paramount consideration should be serving the interests of the country, not adhering to a principle, no matter how fervently held. The better angels of one's political make-up should prevail.

But since the current swearing-in of members of congress doesn't evidently suffice, many observers now feel it's time for a new measure to insure that politicians can function with a full range of independent thought and action and not be weighed down by a slavish fidelity to a certain principle.. A separate pledge should be instituted as soon as possible. Unfortunately, it would have a negative ring to it. The exact wording hasn't been worked out yet, with this phrasing subject to the very compromise it purports to protect.

One version has it: "I hereby abjure any pledges, other than the pledge of allegiance, that might affect my work and decisions in Congress."

Some felt the word "abjure" was too esoteric and that some members might not even know what it means. "Forswear" was felt to be too medieval. More modern words were considered to be more acceptable. The word "renounce" was put forward but was rejected for sounding too harsh. "Recant" came across as too legalistic. "Yield" was already part of congressional usage such as when one surrendered the platform to address Congress. Some words like "relinquish, discontinue, and waive" struck many as too wishy-washy. "Give up" and "deny" were considered too prosaic and trivial-sounding to capture the meaning of the pledge.

Finally, after a good deal of semantic wrangling, it was decided to employ two words: "reject" and "abandon." Both words were designed to show that one was doing more than just putting aside the reason for the original pledge.

Establishing such a pledge would require a bill to be conceived. Finding sponsors for such legislation in both the House of Representatives and the Senate may be chancy and opposition to such a measure is certainly anticipated. A public relations campaign to get people to write to their representatives and ask for their support of such a proposed pledge isn't realistically expected to exert much influence.

If such a bill is drafted and presented to Congress, it would take a majority vote in both chambers. Hopefully, no one – with Tea Party enthusiasts the likely culprits – would filibuster an up and down vote. Presumably, the president would sign the bill.

Given these hurdles, some proponents suggest making the taking of this pledge voluntary at this time. See who agrees to have an open mind while serving the nation and who doesn't, and then make sure their decision is brought up when they face reelection.

Some really meaningful political campaigns might ensue.

84 – A "Nothing" Museum

The U.S. has many museums covering an amazing spectrum of subjects including a Voodoo Museum in New Orleans and the National Atomic Museum near Albuquerque. Some other esoteric subjects which have museums dedicated to them take in forensics, fly-fishing, magic, quilting, dentistry, espionage, police, veterinary medicine, guns, civil rights, D-day/World War II, Kentucky Derby, etc. Presidential museums are popular and bound to grow as each ex-president now will probably be disposed to such a facility dedicated to him or her. Historical museums like the National Underground Railroad Freedom Center in Cincinnati and museums depicting the horrors of the Holocaust in Washington D.C. and Los Angeles have a steady flow of visitors.

Museums galore.

One topic not covered that might be added to this eclectic mix is nothing. That's right. A museum devoted to covering the concept of nothing. The subject is more comprehensive than one might think.

How has "nothing" evolved in our civilization? Who were the first people or society to consider the meaning of "nothing?" And how did they express what they felt or thought about this aspect of their lives? How did the concept of zero get started, and how has it affected our lives, mathematically and otherwise? How have variations of "nothing" and "zero" been used in politics, literature, entertainment, wedding vows, drugs, and a truly amazing roster of both everyday and arcane subjects.

Consider American political history where the "Know Nothing Party' developed and died in the mid 19th century.

In the literary world, there have been countless books, fiction and nonfiction, which employed nothing or zero in their titles and in their narratives. In "Tale of a Tub" by famous satirist Jonathan Swift, his anti-hero wanted "to write about nothing." Philosophers made sure of the concept of nothing in their treatises. One example is the philosophy of nihilism.

Movies, television, and even video games all utilize the nothing variations in their titles. The drug scene features the "just say no" campaign. Astronomy refers to the void and nothingness. Justices of the peace conducting a wedding may still say, "Let no man put asunder…"

Our everyday vocabulary is crowded with expressions that relate to nothing starting with the words "no" and "not." "Negative" comes into play. Among recognizable expressions are: "Nothing doing. Not on your life. Nothing of the kind. Never. He's a non-entity." And there are surely more examples.

How did these expressions arise? Slang is also part of the vocabulary mix, with such words as "zilch" and "goose egg."

Tracing the history of commonplace words and expressions, and their assorted usages, will lend themselves to many worthy displays. The possible range of overall exhibits could easily cover several floors.

Location of such a museum obviously means selection of a major city as a lesser city might deflate its appeal. Washington D.C., on the charge of nothing much being accomplished by our politicians in the nation's capital, is the favorite of many supporters of such a new museum. Many feel the museum would subsequently have sister museums in other countries, showing the common nothing link all nations share one way or another.

While some might think such a museum as being too negative, or trivial, this is far from the case. Visitors to such a museum, if one were created, would likely experience a variety of emotions in learning how the concept of nothing enters their lives – both in a positive and negative way.

85 - Mental Health Centers

Some health maintenance organizations offer Urgent Care, places you can go to see a doctor without an appointment to your regular physician, and when what's bothering you isn't serious enough to go to a hospital emergency room. They serve a valuable purpose in handling such problems as cuts involving relatively simple stitches, bee stings and other insect bites, and a variety of disorders. If the attending doctor thinks further diagnosis and treatment is necessary, they can then suggest a visit to a hospital's emergency room.

Comparable centers should be set up for everyone, with their main purpose being mental health.

What's needed are centers which specialize in restoring or bolstering one's bedrock belief in the logical underpinnings of society, and faith in the basic good will and common sense of governing bodies. Few could argue that for many people such faith, once generally accepted, has been chipped away by a continual succession of scandals, negligence, incompetence, and sheer intransigence by purported leaders. Occasional bouts of disillusionment can be handled before they turn into longer lasting and potentially dangerous malaises. Prevention is the key.

Such centers should be open to everyone and not on a HMO basis. No appointments needed, and with help available on a walk-in basis. There may be a minimal cost for HMO members going to one of their health centers. A minimal charge could be levied all visitors on the same basis. The important element would be providing a center for restoring faith in the concept that good governance is somehow a given and that intelligent decisions by our leaders will surely be made and implemented. Funding could come from a partnership between the federal and state governments. A visit would not come under Medicare and thus avoid adding to the system's costs.

Doctors at these centers would need some additional training in psychology in order for them to assess the needs of visitors and determine if there's a deeper problem that can't be put right with some reassuring words that the world and country still stand on a logical base. Such centers wouldn't involve attempts to psychoanalyze someone in one relatively short session. There would be confidentiality, of course; but just as with a regular visit to a psychiatrist on an individual or group therapy basis, there would a responsibility to warn the authorities if someone expressed a desire to kill a particular person or people in general. Access to such easily available centers for this purpose might well deter the shooting tragedies that deranged people have inflicted on society.

As a precaution against disturbed patrons going amok before palliative measures could be implemented, these centers would be allowed to have a duly-registered gun – not an assault weapon – on their premises.

Topics could encompass a wide range of subjects, stemming from current headlines as well as traditional subjects. No subject would be considered too remote or distasteful to discuss. Probing into a visitor's mindset would be more than cosmetic but hardly surgical in nature. Just an impartial opportunity to put deep-seated or nagging concerns into words can serve to help many people, at least on a temporary basis.

Until such centers are established it's impossible to judge how many people would make use of them and how effective they might be. But it's expected that the volume would start slowly but then expand substantially. A public relations campaign would direct attention to the program. Every effort would be made to avoid any sort of stigma to be attached to such a visit if it were unexpectedly to be disclosed in some fashion. Privacy and confidentiality would be the cornerstones of such centers, so people wouldn't fear any undue publicity.

The theme would be that we all tend to have an ebb and flow of our beliefs on what makes the world go around. Some people may just need a little shoring up while others might require a stronger overhaul of basic values. Naturally, the attending doctor would be in a position to recommend further treatment if a person seemed excessively disillusioned.

The mental health of the public has received insufficient attention. The tragic shooting incidents around the country by troubled individuals have certainly alerted everyone to the mental health issue. But we should deal with normal people as well who have possibly lost some elements in their mental armatures but who aren't candidates for sustained treatment and who aren't a danger to society or themselves.

Providing a professional audience to let off steam, if nothing else, might be a worthy preventive measure to bring about greater mental health and stability.

Here is an idea whose time should come.

Jack Adler

86 - New Tort: Mental Adverse Possession

Adverse possession, in real estate parlance, means that someone can take over property as his or her own once it has been abandoned for a specific amount of time. In our dubious era of many real estate foreclosures, there have been numerous incidents of people taking over homes the owners have had to surrender. Then it's left to the banks usually to handle any dispossessions by those who just have the audacity to move in as if the houses were theirs.

Now some enterprising and creative innovators want to establish mental advance possession as a tort or at least to allow a party to secure a restraining order if they can provide sufficient cause. Legal cases would certainly burgeon, and the attorneys' bank accounts would get a boost.

In effect, such a new tort or semi-tort would allow claims that someone had succeeded in taking a meaningful stake in a person's mind by implanting, one way or another, negative and injurious material. Some may liken this sort of possession as a kind of brainwashing. The material said to be the causative factor could come about through printed or spoken avenues of expression. Widening the scope of possible claims, the material in question would not be needed to be directly expressed to the claimant.

Conceivably, restraining orders in some instances could be given by judges to prevent further damage to one person or the public at large. However, if the accused party hadn't shown overt prejudice against someone, it might be difficult to obtain a restraining order.

Providing proof of actual and potential damage would be quite tricky, but clever lawyers are expected to find ways to establish a cause of action and to win cases.

The rules of evidence may come in for some expansion. Similarly, the range of possible remedies would need a good deal of study. Assessing actual and even punitive damages would be dicey. Specialists in jury selection would clearly need to expand their skills.

It would be clearly understood that alleged cases of demonic possession calling for exorcism wouldn't be part of this emerging legal scenario. Nothing metaphysical is involved.

The major issue then comes down to one of proof. How do you establish grounds for such a legal case?

Suppose a woman in a relationship with a lover felt that a rival had provided material, truthful or otherwise, about her lover in her mind that would eventually cripple her romantic or marital prospects. Imagine a man angling for promotion at his office who is convinced by someone that another aspirant to this position has whispered damaging information to his or her boss? Think of someone claiming that a would-be friend, a secret sympathizer to terrorist causes, managed to plant unpatriotic thoughts in his mind.

Daily private and public life would obviously afford many instances where someone might feel aggrieved in this fashion. To prevent an undue infusion of such cases, which could clog an already strained roster of court cases, this legal claim would probably include a proviso that would mean a financial penalty for asserting a frivolous claim.

However, parties suspecting foul intentions couldn't very well insist on any interrogation. Why would someone admit to having negative thoughts or opinions about others? Use of any truth serum would never be sanctioned. In some cases, people might not even know they had been infected or infested with noxious material.

What's been advanced then, instead of a tort or reason for seeking a restraining order, is a new judicial order: notification and watch. Notification would mean the person was told they were under scrutiny and for what reason. The "watch" would signify that this scrutiny involved specific checks. Athletes are checked periodically to see if they have taken prohibited drugs. In the same way, people can be asked, at preordained periods, how they feel about a person or issue.

Whether such treatment violated constitutional rights would depend, most likely, on a Supreme Court decision.

Detractors also assert that such a legal option would mean that our society, already heavily litigious, would only become more so.

It's time for a new Latin expression to join "Res ipsa loquitur-The thing speaks for itself." Perhaps: "The thing inside can speak for itself - maybe."

87 – False Inspiration From Books

There have been a number of recent cases of readers suing publishers and authors for nonfiction books whose inspirational aspects were subsequently tarnished by revelations that not everything in the books was wholly accurate.

The most recent case probably concerns the books of Lance Armstrong, who finally confessed that his bicycle racing triumphs were fueled by using drugs that he had stoutly denied taking before. Other books brought into some alleged disrepute include *A Million Pieces of Light* and *Three Cups of Tea*, each said to have embellished the author's experiences to some extent.

Publishers have been held to account in some cases. More printings of books have been stopped and copies perhaps recovered from outlets. But often proving damage to one's psyche by discovering what they read wasn't exactly so is a daunting task.

Accordingly, some concerned readers are setting up what constitutes a class action group in readiness. Members of this contingent will be charged with reading new nonfiction books, especially those with supposedly uplifting themes, and determining if there is cause for an intensive fact check that goes beyond any fact checks performed by publishers themselves. If a consensus emerges that a book has taken excessive mind-altering liberties with the facts that could adversely affect readers, then a built-in class action group might already exist to take legal action.

Some have considered this notion to be a sort of literary entrapment scheme. Arguments have also been raised that one could easily challenge the Bible on this basis.

Adherents maintain that their program would only pertain to new books, and only to those that focus on personal experiences and events, and not dogmas or tenets.

The aspect of religious belief might be sticky, both sides agree. A book could expound on one's devotion to a creed, which is one thing, while citing literal events in books like the Bible, that might be challenged. Most people agree books with religious themes shouldn't be part of this literary mix.

Publishers, obviously, aren't too thrilled with this development. They have the big pockets and could ostensibly face more suits with more payouts. The program, however, would be a great boost to the work and careers of fact checkers. They'd be busier than ever before with more at stake.

Authors wouldn't be all that pleased either as they would be held to a more stringent standard than what might have been set before. Publishers do check out books, but it isn't possible to ascertain every claim. On the other hand, any book that passed such an unofficial review would be a useable marketing tool for both authors and publishers. A publisher might conceivably even put a sticker or other notice on a new title that the book had passed muster with this group, just as restaurants put signs on their windows that they've been classified as clean et al.

In the same vein, if the book was bought by movie/television producers, they might also make sure of this group's imprimatur.

Obviously, attorneys wouldn't suffer with the possibility of more class action suits.

The prospect of this plan becoming a chilling factor in the output of first-person, autobiographical books is considered a slim one. Writers with stories to tell will continue to express themselves. The point, group adherents contend, is to insure that providing vivid and engaging copy doesn't become too inventive.

The jury is still out and how successful this program would prove to be. No name has yet been given to this group of inchoate literary whistleblowers. Among those thrown out thus far are: Concerned Citizens for Literary Truth (CCLT), Tell It As It Is (TIAIS), and Cooked Books (CB). More entries are expected, and the public has been invited to contribute their ideas.

88 - Taking A Political Break

Well-founded complaints about the prolonged and frantic struggle to raise funds for political campaigns have led to a radical concept being floated around.

The idea concerns members of the House of Representatives now but a way may be found eventually to extend the putative plan to the Senate.

House members are elected for two-year periods. This time span leads these politicians to quickly start tending to campaign treasure chests in advance of seeking renomination by their party and then reelection if they do run again. Seeking money for the next campaign is an entrenched part of the political process.

Accordingly, it's felt by many observers – from all political parties and points of view - that an excessive amount of time and effort is spent by representatives in raising money rather than working on legislation that serves the nation and their constituents. This financial drive has become even more of an issue with the recent, and troublesome, decision by the Supreme Court allowing corporations more leeway to bestow lucre on their favored candidates.

Other than new court decisions overturning this mistake, and courageous legislation by Congress, which both seem unlikely, the theory now is to limit candidates to one two year term at a time. After this term ends they can't run again for another two years. Essentially, they would be compelled to take a two-year break. However, they can run for office again after this break period ends.

If the program is enacted, and works as expected, members should be able to really concentrate on why they were elected without the substantial distractions that inevitably occur if they're raising reelection money at the same time they are supposed to be working on needed legislation. Their attention wouldn't be divided so drastically. They can also use the two-year break before they run again to focus on money for their future television commercials and other campaign costs.

Members would be held to strict adherence to desist from fundraising during the period they are in office. Failure would mean being hauled before the Ethics Committee or even risking expulsion from the House.

One of the arguments against this proposal is that members would lose their position on various committees and the chance to eventually lead key committees. The experience and knowledge that they gain in the first two years would be in hiatus for the next two years, depriving the nation and their constituents of their enhanced wisdom and value.

To offset this potential disadvantage, a provision would be made that their standing in any committee wouldn't be lost. If and when reelected, they would be guaranteed a return to their previous standing in any committee's hierarchy.

Meanwhile, it's recognized that the representatives – in addition to fundraising in the intervening two years – would have time to better evaluate their work and voting record. This period of introspection might have a very worthwhile influence on their subsequent political career.

Moreover, rather than spending most of their time in Washington D.C., representatives would be able to devote virtually of this fallow period – to borrow an agricultural term – to establish even closer ties to their community. Obviously, such stronger connections to potential voters would invigorate their chances for renomination by their own party and then success in the general election.

Getting approval for such a major change in our political system is problematical. Vested interests would doubtless resist such an upheaval.

But the time has come for a serious review. Were a national referendum held on the subject by the public, the result would probably favor such a shake-up.

Don't be surprised to see people asking you to sign petitions at supermarkets.

89 - Minimum Wage Blues

Attempts to raise the minimum wage level will always face steep challenges from many in the business community. In addition to other drawbacks to such a hike, business leaders argue that paying more to employees will lead to hiring less employees and higher prices.

This argument, others hold, is specious. Bringing more people up economically will increase demand, productivity, and the need for more employees.

Regardless, on how one falls out on this issue, there are other possible ways to improve the working conditions of the millions of low wage earners in the U.S. Given any breakthrough on the immigration issue, this number will only expand.

Accordingly, a plan being discussed covers extra benefits that can be provided to minimum wage employees in lieu of a boost in their hourly pay. Some of the provisions will doubtless be controversial, but at least they will be brought before the public eye – and perhaps the public conscience.

Such employees can certainly be given more generous free or heavily discounted products. If items are involved, such as at stores, employees can probably get much needed clothing and household goods, thus saving them the expense of buying these items and at usually marked up prices. If a food-serving place is involved, then minimum wage earners should be accorded even more free meals than they might be getting now. Even take-home meals could be provided.

Despite their lowly status on the economic hierarchy, these employees might also be provided some sort of profit sharing program. The amount may be modest, but the idea of being part of the company's progress and a share in the economic motor of the U.S. would give them a source of national and company pride. Clearly, such an advantage coming to newly minted citizens, courtesy of any resolution of the immigration problem, would be especially meaningful to this group. However, the influx of such new citizenry would be quite a few years in the offing.

Other than money, nothing may give low wage employees more of a surge of hope for their rise on the economic ladder than a chance to provide input to the company. If no union is involved, let a representative of these employees sit in on management meetings and be given an honest opportunity to present their opinion on any subject on the agenda. The results of such commentary, from such an unexpected quarter, might prove more commercially useful than anticipated. Indeed, some employees might advance to higher paid positions in fairly quick order. In which case, they should be succeeded by another minimum wage earner. The process should be ongoing.

Having a share in the company's bottom line would give these employees a tremendous incentive to provide even greater productivity.

If there are a minimum number of low wage earners – with this amount still to be determined – they should be given a place to meet on a regular basis on company ground and possibly even during company time.

Employees might be given extra days off, and shown much more leeway in time off for personal needs. If any probationary periods are applied to new-hires, these periods should be reasonably lessened. Companies could even offer after-work classes in English and

American history on a need-to-know basis for newcomers to the U.S. Immersion in the economic system needn't be limited to just work.

All these measures, cumulatively, would be a wise investment by employers. Their profits would probably show some modest increase, and all without presidential prodding or congressional legislation. The cost of these provisions would be slight in relation to the benefits to both employers and low wage employees. The lifestyle and general economic standing of minimum wage earners would certainly be enhanced.

Supporters of the program are so sure of its merit that they're looking for congressional sponsors. None, unfortunately, have been found yet.

90 – Political Betting Pools

Betting pools are as intrinsically American as apple pie and barbecues. But applying the concept to the political arena is a new twist. Such pools may go beyond simple office pools and be expanded to cover major political issues. As projected, the new pools would be conducted on a state-by-state basis. Not all states would necessarily find the pools to their taste. But states that have lotteries and other gambling venues are likely to at least experiment with the program.

.Sample issues would revolve around major debates in Congress over elections, budgets, foreign relations, confirmation of Cabinet positions, appointment of new Supreme Court justices, et al. Given the nature of partisan politics in Washington D.C. there would be ample issues for one to bet when they might be resolved and what the resolution might be. .

Opposition to the pools centers more around disrespect for the country's political process than expanding the amount of gambling that already goes on. Proponents contend that the political betting pools wouldn't be unpatriotic. Instead, the pools would, in their way, cultivate more interest in political issues and exercise a strong educational impact. Civic interest, not very high, would grow. Apathy, much too high, would diminish. Some adherents go even further by arguing that such political pools are another element of our great American democracy. One can show solid interest in significant debates, even in this less conventional fashion. The system is likely, they claim, to become a standard feature in the near future. In fact, supporters suggest that the break-down of bets would inevitably come into play during political campaigns. Indicators of public support, derived from betting patterns, could become talking points in campaign speeches, brochures, and other collateral material that clutter campaigns.

The motto or creed of pool proponents revolve around the proposed system representing another demonstration and model of American ingenuity and enterprise.

Many disagree, arguing that other countries, and cultures, might construe such betting pools as another example of American depravity and decadence and use these charges to drum up support against the Great Satan. The hope, and that's all it can be at this juncture, is that people that think the U.S. is dissolute would only feel more so; but few minds would likely be changed by Americans, who already gamble, wagering on still another subject.

Another point often invoked contends that betting on politics is at least a step up from playing poker or other games of chance.

Perhaps putting too rosy a face on the subject pool planners believe that such pools represent a degree of political maturity that could well serve as a role model for other nations. Obviously, the jury is out both domestically and internationally on whether such pools can start and then prosper.

Many of the pools might turn out to be short-lived. Others could easily last for longer periods. Minimum and maximum amounts that could be wagered would be established on the basis that everyone from any economic quarter could participate. No one would suffer any significant dent to his or her wallet; nor would wealthier betters be able to dominate. In this vein, no one would go into debt through lack of discipline and excessive gambling like take place with depressing consistency at casinos in Las Vegas and other venues.

Some of the money naturally would have to go to the state to defray the cost of administration. But this tab could be lessened considerably by the state paying unemployed people to handle the system. However, a state supervisor would provide final control. Winners would receive the same amount based on their bets.

In addition to determining acceptable on-site places to lodge bet, ways to conduct the betting pools online are also being explored.

A new wave of gambling may be upon us.

91 - National Shun Association

At first blush, everyone is likely to take the National Shun Association, or NSA, as a take-off on the NRA or National Rifle Association. Some might confuse the NSA with the National Security Agency as they share the same initials, too. Actually, there is an element of security involved with the Shun members. Through Shun you can receive a large measure of protection from the political pressures the rifle folks exert on elected officials to follow their preferred policies. These politicians will learn that if they consistently vote the "guns are great" way their reelection chances may be dimmed, even if their coffers remain filled with "donations."

In effect, the NSA would serve as a bulwark against anyone or any organization trampling on the legitimate, logical but not necessary legal rights of the American public. Far from being a special interest itself, the NSA would be an antidote to special interests. No entity would be immune from the NSA searchlight. While likened in some cases to a sort of boycott, shunning would be more suggestive and less controlling.

Unlike other organizations with imposing offices and salaried staff the NSA would impose a modest annual dues of only $1. Its message will be sent out by email, thus saving a good bit of money. Only a few dedicated members will be required to handle day-to-day work which would doubtless call for research. Much as the Wikipedia site on the Internet is fueled by volunteers, the NSA can be aided by people willing to contribute their time and efforts for a good cause.

Members of the NSA won't be compelled to follow the recommendations made by a 12- member board composed of prominent people from a variety of fields. A two-thirds vote would be needed to pass any specific shun directive.

Establishing the NSA will not be easy. The public may be dubious, subject already to an avalanche of influences; but the more they learn about the association the more, backers say, they'll support it. Late night comics might play around with "shunsters" cracks, but even that rigmarole would further entrench the association in the public eye. A certain number of courtesy comments can be expected by top governmental officials, eager to show their hearts if not their pockets are in the right place.

Examinations of the NSA in practice would soon follow and do even more to alert the public to the association's value.

Let's use the case of a congressman we'll call Harvey Hasbent from an unnamed state. He wants, of course to be reelected. American politics being what it is he has to start collecting money for reelection campaign almost as soon as he's sworn in. Two years for the congressional term passes very fast. The goodly gun folk supported his first term, but if he wants their continuing support he'll have to toe the line. A crucial gun control bill emerges in Congress. The NRA wants a certain no vote. Now, let's look at what's at stake for Congressman Hasbent should he have the audacity to vote his conscience and do what's best for the American people. Not only might he lose financial support from the NRA, he would face the formidable marketing campaign that might be waged against him to convince his constituents of his fall from favor. Many an elected official, fearful of this onslaught on their political fortunes, have voted accordingly.

Can the NSA actually turn the tide?

In this same scenario, the NSA wouldn't be able to assist Hasbent financially. But it could effectively counter adverse marketing/mailings et al with its own commentary complimenting Hasbent on his stalwart stand. At the very least, this conflicting judgments and recommendations on how to vote on an issue/bill would lessen the NRA's clout, and help constituents see a more balanced perspective. The cost to the NSA would be minimal; the benefit to Hasbent substantial; the advantage to the public, enormous.

Politics is just one area of possible shun use. Members might be able exert pressure on telemarketers (if you can gain their identity), manufacturers of dubious products, producers of excessively prurient and violent entertainment, etc.

There's no guarantee that this type of shunning will work. But movements start small, and then gather steam. Give it a try.

Let's start shunning!

92 – Celebrity Monarchy

The U.S. has many show business celebrities but no monarchy. Some persons contend we pay too much attention to the former and don't need the latter.

But the reality is that we're inundated with an excess of celebrities or near celebrities from every form and branch of entertainment. This is particularly noticeable on television when so and so is trumpeted as a major figure viewers should ostensibly know about. This is far from the case. Many television viewers are uncertain who is actually being cited or interviewed on various shows, including news programs. With the blurring of distinction between hard news and entertainment-related material, the problem of immediate recognition of names and faces becomes a growing factor. The same uncertainty pertains to print media as well.

Some help may be on the way through creation of a "celebrity monarchy" or "show business nobility" roster that would give viewers a hint of how famous and important the show business luminary was even if they don't recognize the name and aren't a fan of the particular genre (if the genre is, hopefully, cited). For example, not everyone is a fan of rock or country music. A committee of knowledgeable show business enthusiasts, with no commercial ties to any entertainer, would be entrusted in determining what title should be given to each personality.

In coming up with a roster of potential titles, the initial thought was to invent distinctively American titles that corresponded to known titles of royalty. But then it was decided a new set of titles might be too confusing and take too long to settle in. Accordingly, familiar terms would be used.

As proposed, the titles of king and queen wouldn't be used as too imposing. Prince and princess would be reserved for award winners in any sphere of entertainment, and there's no shortage of ceremonies to present such honors. The second range of titular recognition would go to entertainers who were runner-ups in any sort of award ceremony or competition. These personalities would get the designation of duke and duchess.

The process gets dicier with the remainder of the many fine performers in the entertainment world. Some entertainers are clearly better known than others. Some performers may be active in more than one type of entertainment, such as an actor who also directs films or a writer who also acts. In this light, there is some thought to a separate title being set aside for hybrid performers such as count and countess.

Entertainers who have been professionals for at least five years would be eligible to receive the titles of and baron and baroness. The distaff term might be changed to avoid any suggestion that the female entertainer was barren.

In this fashion the titles would signify the personality had achieved a sufficient record of accomplishment in their specific field of entertainment to merit "noble" attention.

No one doubts that it will take the public some time to become familiar with these levels of celebrity monarchy. But eventually television viewers would have an easier time appreciating the attention given to personalities that don't immediately register with them.

A poll would be taken of entertainers to ascertain their feelings about the entire program and their individual title. If an entertainer didn't want a title, or felt a different title was deserved, their wishes would be taken into consideration. No one would be compelled to use the title in whatever description they gave of themselves. Overall, it's felt that entertainers would welcome the honor and recognize the need for its creation.

In the future, the hope is that celebrity monarchy will mean that statements like "Who's he?" and "I never heard of her" will be less spoken or thought than before. Unfamiliarity with some entertainers will obviously persist, but at least viewers will know more precisely whose names and personas are being thrust upon them with their morning coffee.

93- Emotional Age Vs. Chronological Age

We're accustomed to using our chronological age when disclosing how old we are. Normally, when asked one's age, a truthful answer is given on important forms like taxes, employment, et al. Obviously, there are other social occasions when one may be less disposed to reveal their age. Now with demographic data showing the increasing aging of the population, some sentiment has emerged for another age-related response that might be used in social circumstances.

It's a truism that people age differently but this reality needs to be taken into greater consideration today, especially with the increasing number of "old-olds" in our society. Someone who is 80 may come across as someone who is actually that age or even seem older. Conversely, an 80-year old person might appear to be more like a sprightly 60-year old. Chronological age, while a verity, still doesn't adequately illumine someone's make-up and deportment. Other than physical and health considerations, which aren't to be slighted, there can be a considerable difference. Others might not want to take note, but the individual could well feel a significant aspect of their persona was being left out or ignored.

Consequently, we have an inherent right to present an alternative age that might better represent our social personality. Accordingly, a movement is taking place to establish this other "age" as our "emotional age" or "EA."

In the future, one might cite one's CA – chronological age – as well as emotional age or EA. Where legal matters come into play, chronological age will still be paramount. Clearly, in any social setting, people would have more of a choice.

Choosing not to supply one's chronological age may be seen as a vanity-related dodge, and sometimes it probably would be. But that's no reason to deny people a chance to present themselves in a different light and let others choose whether EA is a better clue to the person and their intrinsic attitude about themselves and life in general.

Determining one's emotional age is obviously quite subjective. Whereas chronological age is fixed, one's emotional age can vary from day to day depending on personal circumstances. Criteria that one might use to assess their EA include what entertainment they like; what television shows do they watch; do they like to travel, and if so, with others on a guided tour or to wander on an independent basis; are they willing to sample new foods, etc. The key would be the degrees of willingness and desire to still learn new things and to have new experiences. No one is the same in these regards. Some people are more adventurous than others.

No one answer would provide a clear-cut answer. But cumulatively they can probably shed light on one's emotional state.

Dating, even among the aged, may take on another scope if EA catches on as expected. People, women especially perhaps, tend to be reluctant to divulge their ages. But now use of EA can provide another response. At the very least, it would inject an interesting component to many conversations.

No one is likely to automatically accept another's opinion of themselves that comes with citing an EA. People can certainly cite a younger EA than seems plausible. Shedding years from one's chronological age will always be suspected with expressions of hopefully polite wonder. This type of reaction, of course, will especially be a calculation in social exchanges. How one handles EA will probably be a good subject for advice offered by etiquette columnists, and an outpouring of new advice books can be expected.

However, adding age-related spice to how we engage with other people might add a lively dimension that could revitalize many lives. The aging process, as well as social niceties, may never be the same.

Make EA work for you!

Jack Adler

94 – The New Machismo

Mark the new machismo!

Bulging biceps, a flat stomach, and all the other muscular elements that show a striking physicality are being bypassed by a new kind of toughness. The times change, and both men and women, now have to recalibrate their impressions of male looks and behavior. What brought admiring looks from women, and envious glances from other men, may now have far less of an impact in the dance between the sexes as well as other social and business related encounters and situations.

Flaunting raw strength now is more likely to generate an impression of raw and undeveloped character.

The new machismo centers more on an inner mental strength that has to be shown by external efforts, either by word or deed. One can only be accorded all the respect due a really strong personality by clearly disdaining a physical show of force and instead showing a courageous brand of behavior that defies stale custom and tradition and forges new trails of thought and action.

Instead of bulking up now, by spending hours of grueling workouts at gyms, men feel a need to show their mettle by bold gestures and ideas. But these measures, radical or otherwise, have to be sensible and stem from an extensive knowledge of the world's affairs. Far more than in the past, machismo has come to mean an ability to both show knowledge and ways to use this information constructively.

Accordingly, men are now more disposed to read a newspaper a day and not depend on television to learn about daily events. Visits to libraries and museums have become more frequent and intensive. Subscriptions to magazines offering news and opinions has grown substantially.

However, the drive to have and express more familiarity with world events doesn't mean one has to become an intellectual or a bookworm. There is no threat of being considered a nerd or anything of that cruel nature.

Not at all.

Guidebooks for mastering the new machismo are beginning to be written and published. There's no one proven and tried method as this subtle cultural change has woven itself into the social fabric without great fanfare. Some trial and error should be anticipated. One doesn't have to blurt out striking new ideas about politics, trouble spots around the globe, religion, medicine, or any major or minor topic. Nor should one feel obligated to utter words of infinite wisdom, or to come with marvelous new solutions to problems bedeviling leaders in every field of endeavor.

The key concept of the new machismo now reverts to the dictum: by their words and deeds shall you know them.

The new man wants to be known for what he shows he knows, and how he can creatively use his knowledge, and not by how he fills out his clothing.

Instead of insipid chatter about nothing of consequence, say at a first date, a man might be more disposed now to let the lady know right away where he stands on the Middle East situation, unrest in Myanmar, the Chinese economic rise, and any number of other outstanding issues. What should be done, when, and by whom? Recognition of such stalwart declarations would likely usher in a look of genuine admiration and perhaps the start of a meaningful relationship.

Similarly, imagine yourself in any situation where brawn might have been the decisive factor in the past, and now how you can employ a new and more powerful weapon: your mind.

The new machismo is catching on, and the sooner men make needed adjustments, the better. Attitude has become more important than anatomy. Be more concerned with the pulse of the world than your pectoral shape. You can still eat red meat and not be a vegetarian. Nor do you have to keep an assault weapon in your closet.

Just be aware that masculinity isn't what it used to be. Mirrors can lie.

95 – Outdated Movie/TV Scenes

Fed up with standard departures from reality in movie and television fare, a group of disgruntled watchers hope to petition producers and studios, as well as writers, to cease using some obvious ploys and to come up with more realistic scenes that accurately match real life.

One representative example of key sequences deplored is having curtains or blinds open so the authorities or criminals alike can peer in and see who is in the room and what they are doing. In real life, it's argued, people would surely have their curtains or blinds drawn, especially if any intimacy is involved. How many people undress, or make love, so visibly from outside? How many scenes have you seen with an attractive woman disrobing in full sight in her own apartment or bedroom and then discreetly entering a shower? How many women are so indifferent to who gets to admire their figures?

Another common cinematic tactic criticized comes when a criminal holding a gun or weapon on someone, usually someone in law enforcement but not always, is made to come so close to the good guy that he can lunge forward and knock the gun or knife aside. In real life, a criminal – at least a professional one – wouldn't be so stupid, negligent or foolhardy to get that near his victim or target. Yet this type of scene is omnipresent in action flicks.

How often does a scene involve someone fleeing a pursuing car? The intended victim, for reasons defying common sense, keeps running in a straight direction in front of the auto rather than immediately dodging to the left or right. Even in the fury of the moment, most people wouldn't stay in the car's headlights in this fashion if they had the time to move aside.

The woman-in-peril situation is often overdone. One illustration: having the woman wander into some dark and dangerous neighborhood without any greater justification for taking this route.

There are other numerous examples of such convenient dismissal of what would likely take place in real life situations. The usual purpose is to show physical action primarily. Violence, mayhem, and a prodigious amount of blood shedding remain cardinal elements of both movies and television shows. Suspension of belief is often accomplished to present what is considered a reasonable entertainment. But times are changing along with public perceptions. New and younger audiences, the group argues, have grown tired of scenes defying the common sense of the situation. Many jaded viewers, while not seeking monumental changes, would welcome more sensible scenes.

The group doesn't want to limit creativity factors, and it recognizes that action is essential and graphic images attracts viewers and keeps them glued to the television screen. But it does hope to generate more enlightened and realistic portrayals.

Ironically, the group points out that the trend has been to show more of the anatomy of performers, and to allow an infusion of words in dialogue that were once considered taboo, especially on television. Yet stock evasions of reality take place regularly in shows. There hasn't been a parallel development of new tactics or techniques in potentially lethal confrontations, bedroom peering, and chase scenes to satisfy more sophisticated audiences.

The group has made it clear it isn't asking for a change in another common scene where a killer delays his/her dirty deed to take time in explaining what happened to bring about this sorry end. Or the killer allows his or her prey to keep asking questions, which are naturally answered with unbelievable courtesy, thus delaying the critical moment of execution. The killer either moves too close or allows the intended victim to approach; or help arrives in the nick of time. The predictability factor has led to substantial staleness in this sort of denouement.

While such scenes are deemed needed to explain the plot, it may be possible to add to the reality of the encounter through more creative dialogue or even staging.

Coming up with a grass roots campaign to convince the powers-that-be in the entertainment industry won't be easy. Many people are content with what they have. Still, it's felt that the handwriting is on the wall, or in this case, on the screen.

Jack Adler

96 -. Home "Know Yourself" Kit

Sophocles, the ancient Greek philosopher, advised in a famous dictum: *know thyself*. Ralph Waldo Emerson, our much admired 19th century philosopher, espoused the same course. So have other philosophers and commenters on the human condition.

In a turbulent world, mired in threats of war on Earth and marauding meteors from space, many more people are prone to take this advice seriously. In an unsettled world, where many beliefs have been shattered, many wonder about the intrinsic nature of their value system. What do they still believe and why? But they admit they need help in conducting what is clearly an intrinsically private matter. The process of sincere self-examination has proven to be quite difficult for many conscientious and well-meaning people.

Consequently, a group of psychiatrists have devised a test that people can take in the privacy of their own homes which can aid them to assess the directions of their thoughts and beliefs. They can, in effect, discern values and beliefs they cling to which they no longer feel the same comfort with. They may not get any clear-cut or final determinations, but they are expected to shed some outdated notions and secure a clearer look at their own mental make-up.

While not a physical device, this self-administered examination follows in the path of other kits one can use at home for such purposes as determining pregnancy, blood in the stool, etc.

No grades are involved to mark yourself by the number of "right" answers as there would be no right or wrong responses. However, one would be enabled – or so the creators of the test believe – to ponder indications of their patterns or predilections on various subjects. No one else need see the results, and it would be entirely up to the individual how much stock to put in any individual response or the cumulative impact of their answers. Similarly, it would be strictly up to the person to consider any need to consult any sort of specialist – medical, religious, educational, et al. Forewarnings, while probably unnecessary in the great majority of cases, can still be eminently useful and this factor shouldn't be disregarded.

At this point twenty-five questions will be on the test, and one doesn't have to complete the test at one sitting.

Ten questions will be multiple choice. With many multiple choice questions, there are four possible answers, and one or two can often be quickly dismissed. One then decides between the two remaining answers. However, in these multiple choice questions, all four responses will be strong candidates. In a separate paper that one isn't supposed to look at until the test is completed, there will be a rationale for each of the four answers. The one picked by the test user will indicate their leanings.

The other fifteen questions will call for a response that can just be mental, though one can jot down a response and in any length desired. Responses might be one word or a long composition. Many people are likely to skip anything longer than a word or two, or perhaps a short sentence. Accordingly, future versions of the test, based on an initial survey, may trim this section to five questions and add true-false questions instead.

Key questions, often overlapping, will cover politics, religion, morality, ethics, preventive war, torture, governmental lying, congressional cowardice, national debt, generational harmony, drugs, abortion, same-sex marriage, etc. The questions will be updated on a regular basis.

Critics of the test contend that people may not, even with the best of intentions, provide honest answers. Self-deceptions will plague users and work to continue whatever their original perspective were on any particular issue.

The creators, however, believe that the mere desire to take the test indicates a willingness to plumb one's mind.

Pricing for the tests hasn't been set yet but a nominal tab is expected. Distribution will probably be at many stationery stores and stationery sections in department stores.

In the future people may come to even ask someone else in conversation: "Do you know yourself? Have you taken the test?"

97 - Index Of Dubious Items

Given the frequent updating on what foods and other items can be questionable to ingest or otherwise come in contact with, perhaps it's time for a national index on the Internet that can be updated as often as necessary to keep the public on the right track. It's high time for such a single place where the public can seek current information and advice. Such a site listing things that perhaps deserve a taboo status would probably be quite welcome to most people, relieving unnecessary alarums and providing a means to overcome a tendency to simply ignore things when they seem too complicated or subject to change.

With remarkable frequency there are often reports of a new medical finding that suggests that we shouldn't be eating or drinking what we're consuming, or not in the same amounts. It's clearly difficult for most people to keep up with the barrage of news and advice.

The list of potential subjects is probably larger than many people might think.

Sugary drinks, especially those that exceed certain amounts in cups, are one of the latest subjects. Certain candies have come under criticism. Lunch menu items for children at schools have been dissected for poor and less than healthy inclusions.

The threat of diabetes from sugar intake looms large. And, of course, the amount of obesity in the land is a national scandal.

The amount of salt we absorb through processed foods, and our other usage, has come into sharper focus.

Cutting down on red meat is a choice piece of customary advice.

Junk foods continue to occupy supermarket stalls and home cupboards. Trans fats has been excoriated, which doesn't mean it isn't still prevalent. Fast foods are enticing but hardly a way to have a healthy diet or a decent waistline.

Not every item has to be food or a liquid.

The sheer profusion of drugs available, both prescribed and otherwise, is a huge subject. The potential side effects of certain drugs calls for a good deal of revelations.

The dismal consequences of smoking have long been aired. Many people obviously still smoke. Youngsters still think dangling a cigarette from their mouths is sophisticated and smoke due to peer pressure. No matter what dangers are posted on packs of cigarettes, or how much their prices rise, the habit persists. Creation of another place to assert the dangers of cigarette smoking may have no impact, at least not initially. But as this kind of inclusive index, hopefully endorsed by authoritative private and public officials and agencies gathers steam and stature, it may eventually dissuade some people from voluntarily shortening their lives and increasing the chances for various diseases to strike them.

The majority of people now use computers. More disclosures on how close to sit next to screens, carpal tunnel syndrome, and other pitfalls are worthy of coverage.

Loud music can be damaging to one's hearing. Yet noise pollution continues to proliferate. Getting some notion of what the decibel count is on some common noisemakers could help individuals considerably.

The list of subjects could take on deceptive discounts, mail order frauds and other scams, misleading ads and commercials, etc.

Creation of such a list could be entrusted to a public committee composed of health and educational authorities, and this roster could be changed annually to prevent any stagnancy or hardening of viewpoints. Items could be added, deleted or edited at any time. The public would be able to make suggestions. No political, ethnic, or religious references would be allowed.

Printed copies of the index could be made available at many locations including bulletin boards at schools at every academic level. Libraries and even supermarket posting boards might be used. One could simply print the roster off the Internet, and many such print-outs may wind up stuck on refrigerator doors.

No one, of course, would be obligated to honor any suggestion on the index. One could continue following any course considered, index-wise, as unhealthy and unsafe. But the index would surely serve as a steady beacon of positive values. Indeed, many observers feel the index would become a common conversational tool with mothers berating children, spouses cautioning their mates, and advertisers taking stock.

98 - Asymmetric Peace

Much has been written that we're faced with asymmetric warfare for the foreseeable future, a dire situation where groups and individuals from non-states can launch terrorist attacks without the formality of a declaration of war. The growing realization that a cyber attack, which could cripple our infrastructure, is another terrible weapon.

Measures to detect and defuse these lurking threats are a constant priority. Sacrifices in personal freedoms are called for.

But now a dramatic new force is emerging which could put a hopeful perspective on the struggles and rivalries of the world. "Asymmetric Peace" may not bring a total end to terrorism and wars but it should certainly make a sizeable dent.

Education is at the forefront of the program, still in the planning stage and subject to the approval of subscribing nations. A large number of students beginning academic instruction, say at the age five or six, would be mandated to attend school in another country for at least two years. This is considered sufficient time to learn a new language and become immersed in a different culture. Reading the textbooks of the other nation's school system, showing radically different viewpoints about the U.S., can help develop more of a multi-cultural and universal make-up for future citizens of both nations.

One of the key elements of the program, still in the planning stage and subject to the approval of subscribing nations, is in compulsory marriages between two countries. In this light, a certain number of men and women would agree to marry, based on prospects in a pool of eligible mates set up in each country. This number could be put together just on volunteers, though drafts might be necessary to provide the required mass. The program would be annual, and the couples would be married for life. They, and any of their children, would be joint citizens of both nations and could live where they choose in either nation. Divorces would be possible after one year.

The design of this plan is to cement the two countries together by marital ties that would transcend any of their political and cultural differences. Every effort would be made to make the plan as loose in structure as possible.

Creating a pool of manpower to serve in another's country military services may be an even trickier maneuver to set in motion. Under this provision, a certain number of men, and women, would become part of the army, naval or other units. But this would be for a limited time, six months to a year. Fears of military secrets being divulged are sure to be raised but it's felt that none of the men and women – none would be officers - serving in this fashion would be on a high enough level to make off with valuable information.

The morale factor, perhaps slow originally, would surely grow as the program's roots sunk in.

One area that hasn't worked out thus far is sharing computer technology, but it's thought that all the measures would still lead to greater cooperation in this sphere.

Pairing of nations is another problem to surmount. The notion of Israel and Iran both agreeing to this plan seems chancy to say the least. The same is probably true for India and Pakistan. However, it might work out better between Greece and Turkey, who haven't been the best of international buddies; or between Armenia and

Azerbaijan. Sudan and South Sudan might also become a "couple."

Unfortunately, there is no shortage of trouble spots around the world. Long-standing rivalries, plus historic as well as contemporary frictions, would make the international enterprise hard to carry off. But the need is still paramount.

However, critics are decrying Asymmetric Peace as a hopelessly optimistic and idealistic program and one impossible to implement as a practical matter. Some are already denouncing what they term "international shotgun marriages."

Strange times, though, call for strange solutions

99 – Be A Futurist

Be a futurist!

Not professionally, just on a personal basis which doesn't mean only on an interior basis. You can share your perspectives at will, and once you get going on the futurist trail, you probably will.

One doesn't have to possess a Ph. D in futurism to come up with well thought out, eminently sensible, and utterly articulable comments on a wide range of subjects. Presenting your predictions on what life will be like in a decade or two, or next century, or inevitably, is far easier than you might realize. Chances are that you already hold several unexpressed opinions already that simply need to be sharpened into potential speech.

Determining the current extent of your thoughts, and how well developed and defined they are, can be done without inducing a headache. Having an opinion on what you think will happen doesn't necessarily mean that you welcome that outcome – unless you so state it. A perspective just shows a well-rounded mind, not a die-hard exponent of any burning issue.

Some issues are immediately in the public eye so it would be difficult not to have already formulated an opinion. For example, consider same-sex marriage. It seems clear that with or without legal approval, same sex marriage will triumph and probably in a relatively short time. But you can calculate how it will take this cultural changeover to fully become commonplace.

But then you can expand the topic in interesting ways that show your capacity for intelligent prophecy. How far will same sex marriage go? Will a man be legally allowed to have more than one wife (a throwback to Islamic and Mormon beliefs)? Conversely, as a new or novel practice, can a woman have more than one husband? Your consideration of the latter would surely take in the steady rise of women in the workplace and the political arena.

The same subject might also take in group marriages whereby two or more couples share their vows? Will they become the norm, with people sharing households, children, and incomes? The spurting development of robotics can mean marrying our own creations, clothed in flesh or not. And then are the clones, certainly to become omnipresent. Who else will become marriageable? Corporations? Pets? Alien life forms, and this is clearly a subject one can speculate about.

Consider the right-to-die issue. Do you think it's inevitable that will be recognized as a basic right in every state? And how soon?

Abortion is clearly another critical and divisive issue. Will it be finally resolved one way another, and again, how soon?

Do you think it's inevitable that the U.S. will become bi-lingual with everyone expected to be literate in English as well as Spanish?

Internationally, there are a host of intriguing questions. Will there ever be a world body with muscular enforcement options not subject to veto from one or more countries? Can future holocausts be prevented? Can a nuclear conflict be prevented? Will the so-called clash of civilizations between the world of Islam and the West be resolved in a felicitous meshing of cultures and religions?

There are many other serious issues besetting the U.S. and the world. Nor does one have to be limited by what troubles us today. As a futurist you can also divine what problems and practices may come into vogue in days, years, decades and centuries to come.

The future, like space, may have no discernible boundaries that limit our scope of thought. The only limit is your imagination – and willingness to be forthright in expressing your opinions. One must be wary, of course, of not coming across as a sort of know-it-all and would-be prophet.

Practice makes a reasonable imperfect.

Jack Adler

100 - American Deathnauts

New enemies have prompted discussion of new weapons, some so bizarre that they are withheld from public scrutiny for a variety of reasons. One reason, of course, is not alerting other countries as well as non-state opponents like al Qaeda of our intentions. Another is a well-justified fear about the morbidity of a top-secret program under discussion which, if publicized, might unduly alarm the public and possibly spur an undeserved measure of ridicule.

But there is no doubt, observers say, that a military frontier has dawned that deserves more exploration for military and national security purposes. Ever ready to recognize and face new challenges, the Pentagon's "Operation Styx" project has been designed and implemented to harness death, if at all possible, to continue American policies and values in the afterlife – if one should exist.

Soldiers have died for centuries, but the thought now is to possibly find a way to continue their service beyond death. No one knows, naturally, if such a program is remotely possible. Nor will anyone living ever know. But that's no reason, proponents say, not to prepare a contingency program just in case security issues in life continue in any potential afterlife.

If such a prolongation does exist, proponents don't want to see the U.S. put at a disadvantage. The sheer demographics of the subject are an arguing point. The biggest rival to the U.S. today, and doubtless in the future, is China. But China, due to its much greater population – roughly four times more than the U.S. - has a huge jump among its decedents. It's recognized that nationality may not exist beyond death. Memory of loyalty to the country may disappear. Similarly, remembrances of outstanding life issues may vanish.

Certitude about the theoretical underpinnings of the program is impossible to offer as a justification for Operation Styx. . But ignorance is said to be no excuse for a lack of foresight where the security of the country may somehow be involved, even if it is in metaphysical theory. Though working in perpetual darkness, proponents of the program, argue that it would be gross negligence to do nothing. Fear has grown that the Chinese have opened a huge death gap on the U.S. In the same vein, higher birth rates – and hence the death rate – in other countries where elements of the population are hostile to the U.S. is also a consideration. Concern has mounted about the Arab Spring turning into an Arab Winter due to their higher birth rates..

Accordingly, a secret committee of leading thanatologists have been working on a program at the Pentagon to produce the nation's first crop of American deathnauts. "Conquer death as well as space" is the tentative slogan.

Specially-picked candidates willing to undertake after-death responsibilities that may not exist have come from the military as well as those working for the government in other areas. All have terminal diseases, and each is sworn to secrecy, even from their families and loved ones. Their names will never be disclosed. Plans for some sort of posthumous payment to their heirs is being developed. Special medals for our deathnaut heroes may also be designed though their unveiling may not be soon.

It's feared that other nations have been doing research in the afterlife field as well and the U.S. is behind, as it was once in the space race. Accordingly, the program has an equally secret budget to insure that the U.S. is catching up. If there is such a thing as the afterlife, the priority is to assure that the dead are well disposed to living Americans and the U.S.

Our American deathnauts will be official representatives of the U.S. in any way that's possible. However, no intelligence on what's the situation is in the afterlife is anticipated to come from the deathnauts. This lack of concrete information, however, will not stop our top brass from making other contingency plans on use of our deathnauts.

One must think ahead.

####

Jack Adler
6122 Shadyglade Avenue
North Hollywood, CA 01606
jadler@prodigy.net

Also by Jack Adler

California Mystique (Non-Fiction)

Sons and Daughters of THE GOLDEN STATE - California.

A would-be "queen" of California, a Russian lover, a consul and secret agent , a bandit/folk hero, a literary gold miner, a skiing pioneer, California's first "millionaire", and artists and adventurers of all stripes are part of California's exceptionally eventful and colorful history. The lives and exploits of extraordinary and controversial personalities, from pathfinders of yesteryear to contemporary politicians , provide an especially rich and illuminating tapestry of history.

California's early days, its Spanish and Mexican periods, brief independence as the Bear Republic, and then its growth as part of the United States come to vivid and entertaining life with the description of the deeds and misdeeds of key personalities. The ongoing saga of daring and innovative luminaries helps explain the mystique of California and why it has such a storied and charismatic reputation that continues to attract people from the rest of the country as well as the world.

In addition to the detailed descriptions of the many key personalities enriching and exemplifying California's lure, this book provides practical details on memorabilia including places and sightseeing attractions related to each personality.

Seven Seniors (Fiction)
Action, Adventure, Mystery, Suspense, Romance

Seven different seniors, each ensnared in the harsh difficulties of their historical periods which range from ancient Rome to contemporary America, dramatically show a common link of values that bolster them with courage and dignity as they struggle to not only survive but prevail over their terrible problems.

Each senior is faced with a life-altering decision with their dilemmas involving beheadings and a confusion of loyalties in Parthia, Rome's great rival; suffering the cruelty of the Inquisition in medieval Germany; escaping the clutches of Napoleonic intrigue as a reluctant "spy"; venturing on the dangerous journey west to California through Indian territory on a prairie schooner; the irony of elder abuse reversed; and an odd campaign of public service featuring "senior commandos."

The stories of their tribulations and triumphs graphically show the strength and durability of the human spirit that defies age as well as time and geography.

Turnabout (Fiction)
Action, Adventure, Young Adult, Mystery, Suspense

Turnabout is an ironic coming-of-age novel about a 15-year old high school student who inadvertently sees one of his teachers commit a homicide against another teacher and then blackmails this teacher to make him into a better person, academically and socially.

The teacher, meanwhile, also faces a deepening crisis with his wife whose behavior led to the homicide. The escalating blackmail imbroglio creates a tremendous intertwining impact on their lives with dramatic turnabouts. The student gets involved with a wild fellow student who introduces him to the world of sex and drugs. Then he is blackmailed himself by his fast friend to cover up the death of a young call girl from a drug overdose.

Both student and teacher are brought before the police for questioning about drugs and an improper relationship, with their lives and futures in jeopardy. Ultimately, as portions of the truth emerge, each learns from his experiences as their lives are drastically changed by their actions.

Available from W & B Publishers
www.a-argusbooks.com

About Jack Adler

Jack Adler is a Los Angeles-based writer and author of more than twenty nonfiction and fiction books. He has received a grant as a playwright with several Off-Broadway productions. One play has been published. Formerly he was a freelance columnist for the *Los Angeles Times'* travel section. He has taught various writing courses fore UCLA Extension and the Writer's Digest University.

Jack and his wife, Barbro, have two sons.

www.ingramcontent.com/pod-product-compliance
Lightning Source LLC
Chambersburg PA
CBHW071944110426
42744CB00030B/275